The Interview Rehearsal Book

"What better background for writing a first-class interview book than two successful acting careers? Overcoming rejection, building authentic confidence, and selling during the interview are approached in a brand-new way.

"The Interview Rehearsal Book approaches one of life's most terrifying experiences and breaks it down logically so that the fearful-inspired interview process is first understood and then strategically tackled step-by-step."

—Susan Bixler, author of *Take Action!*
and *The* New *Professional Presence*

"What an informative, well-written book. Gottesman and Mauro bring a wonderful new perspective to interviewing in this easily understood, step-by-step format. If you are looking for a job, you can't afford *not* to read it."

—Emily Koltnow, author of
Congratulations! You've Been Fired,
and founder of Koltnow & Company,
an executive recruiting firm

The
INTERVIEW
REHEARSAL BOOK

7 Steps to
Job-Winning Interviews
Using
Acting Skills
You Never
Knew You Had

DEB GOTTESMAN AND BUZZ MAURO

BERKLEY BOOKS, NEW YORK

"I Hope I Get It"
Music by Marvin Hamlisch
Words by Edward Kleban
Copyright © 1975 by Largo Music, Inc. o/b/o American Music Corp. and Wren Music Co.
Copyright renewed.
International copyright secured.
All rights reserved.

This book is an original publication of The Berkley Publishing Group.

THE INTERVIEW REHEARSAL BOOK

A Berkley Book / published by arrangement with the authors

PRINTING HISTORY
Berkley trade paperback edition / March 1999

The Penguin Putnam Inc. World Wide Web site address is http://www.penguinputnam.com

ISBN: 0-425-16686-4

BERKLEY®
Berkley Books are published by The Berkley Publishing Group, a member of Penguin Putnam Inc., 375 Hudson Street, New York, New York 10014.
BERKLEY and the "B" design are trademarks belonging to Berkley Publishing Corporation.

PRINTED IN THE UNITED STATES OF AMERICA
10 9 8 7 6 5 4 3 2 1

ACKNOWLEDGMENTS

WE WISH to thank the following people for contributing their time, expertise, and enthusiasm to this project: Julia Agostinelli, Amy Austin, Lisa Considine, Laura Derrick, Gillian Drake, Michael Gottesman, Velita Johnson, Alane K. Ludin, Roberta Masters-Cullen, Jerry Rehm, Lynn Seligman, and Lauri A. Wood. Special thanks to Roberta Gottesman and Michael Rodgers for their invaluable contributions to the text of "Day Four: Looking the Part"; to William H. Graham, former Chair of the Catholic University of America Department of Speech and Drama, for his wisdom, guidance, and Bic pen story; and to Stephen Daigler and Jeanne Goldberg for outstanding performances in their supporting roles.

It is hard to imagine that we could survive in this world without being actors. Acting serves as the quintessential social lubricant and a device for protecting our interests and gaining advantage in every aspect of life.

—MARLON BRANDO

CONTENTS

L IST OF EXERCISES

*P*ROLOGUE: WHAT ACTORS KNOW AND YOU SHOULD TOO

Who am I anyway?
Am I my resume?
That is a picture of a person I don't know.
What does he want from me?
What should I try to be?
So many faces all around, and here we go.
I need this job.
Oh God, I need this show.

—FROM THE OPENING NUMBER OF *A CHORUS LINE*

WHAT CAN actors teach you about getting a job? A lot more than you might think.

For one thing, no one knows more about finding work than an actor. In some professions landing a good job means you're set for the next ten or fifteen years, but actors know a show may last only a few weeks, and then it'll be time to look for work again.

This book was written by actors for people interviewing in any profession because we have a unique perspective on what it takes to get hired. It's not uncommon for five hundred actors to show up at a Broadway cattle call, all competing for the same role. You're given a two-minute audition slot and in this ridiculously short time you must prove you can do the role better than anyone else. With odds like these, it's no wonder that the actors who get jobs are the ones who know how to make the most of their two minutes.

But if you think actors are the only people who need to learn how to audition, think again. In the business world, the audition is officially known as the job interview, but aren't they really the same thing? The interview is your opportunity to show a potential employer how you might behave in the "role" (the job you're applying for) if you get "cast" (hired by the company). In a very limited amount of time—probably longer than two minutes, but shorter than an hour—an interviewer needs to find out who you are so she can assess how you'll perform in the future.

Nothing is more important in the interview than the actor's specialty: self-presentation. Your skills and qualifications may have gotten you in the door, but it's your personality—the winning way you *present* your skills and qualifications—that will get you the job. You only get one chance to make a great impression, so you've got to let the interviewer see you at your best.

The Interview Rehearsal Book will teach you to use the tools of the actor's trade—personal experience, imagination, and rehearsal—to help you discover the role of your "best self," the you that truly is right for the part.

Yes, it's a role, but that doesn't mean it's phony. Although we may not be aware of it, we all play many roles in our lives: child, parent, student, lover, colleague, friend, and neighbor, to name a few. These roles allow us to express different parts of ourselves in different situations. They're an indispensable part of how we deal with the world. The face we show the mirror in the morning is not the one we show the boss at a meeting, and it's a good thing!

This book will help you to discover all the different facets of the unique individual that you are and to choose the characteristics you want to emphasize in your interview. The role you explore through these exercises will be one that increases your self-confidence, improves your communication skills, diminishes your fears, and prepares you to present your best self to your future employer.

As we say in the business: Break a leg!

The
INTERVIEW
REHEARSAL BOOK

Getting Started

Most books about how to interview for a job (and there are hundreds of them) will list lots of things you should remember to do: look the interviewer in the eye, shake hands firmly, smile, sell yourself, project confidence, etc. Some of the recommendations have merit and others don't, but even the good ideas are usually nothing more than common sense. If a behavior comes naturally to you, what good is reading it in a list? And, more important, if a behavior does *not* come naturally to you, what good is reading it in a list?

One way to learn something is by reading about it. A much better way is by doing it. Interviewing is a physical activity: you do it with your body. Most people would consider it foolish to try to learn to ski or to play the violin by reading book after book and never putting on the boots or picking up the bow. The same goes for interviewing. Practice makes perfect.

The purpose of the book you now hold in your hands is to provide training in a variety of techniques that will actually *give* you the skills other books simply say you should master. As it turns out, the basic principles of acting provide just the techniques you need. In the seven steps of this program you will learn to play yourself the best way you possibly can.

You Are Not Your Resume

The interview is the pivotal event in your job search. It is undeniably true that the job can be won or lost in the time you spend sitting opposite the decision maker. This is because it is only through your live interaction with another human being that the interviewer can see who you really are.

If the most memorable thing an interviewer can recall about you is your resume, it wasn't a very successful interview. The interview is your chance to show who you are beyond what's on the page.

If you think about it, you'll realize that most of the people interviewing for any given job have very similar credentials. The job requires a certain level of education and experience. People who have far more than what's required probably aren't applying for it, and people who have less than what's required probably won't be called in for an interview. So it stands to reason that everyone comes in with basically the same resume.

Even if your resume somehow shows that you've been incredibly successful in your previous jobs, that's no guarantee you'll be a good match for the present position. And the interviewer is looking for just one thing: the right match.

"You Like Me. You Really, Really Like Me."

SOME LIES:

- Whoever has the best resume will get the job.

- The person with the most directly applicable experience will get the job.

- Someone who knows someone at the company will get the job.

One thing is more important than any of your connections, experiences, or accomplishments: Who you are. The interview is the employer's only chance to see you in action. Are you easy to work with? Do you listen well? Are you a person who can stick to a task? The answers to all these implied questions can and should be demonstrated in the interview.

THE TRUTH: Whoever makes the best impression will get the job.

We've found that even interviewers themselves don't always realize how subjective they're being. They almost always think they're hiring the person who is the most objectively qualified, but the one they're really hiring is simply the one they like best. They may not be consciously aware of how much they're being influenced by your self-presentation, but it's always going to make a big difference whether they know it or not.

So, you've entered the job market with certain given experiences and credentials. The next step is to learn how to present yourself in a way that will set you off from the competition.

Contrary to popular belief, interviewing is a skill that can be learned. The reason people don't believe it is that they've read books about it and haven't gotten any better. They haven't gotten better because they haven't practiced. This book will teach you how to practice.

HOW TO USE THIS BOOK

To get the most out of this book, you should begin at the beginning and work your way through to the end. It's a carefully structured, proven system for developing your ability to interview well, and if you commit to doing the whole thing, you're certain to see results. So if you skipped the Prologue, better go back and read it.

The Seven Steps

The rest of this book is composed of seven steps of readings and exercises priming you for a job interview, and a final section that deals with what happens after your seven steps of preparation are completed. The program is most effective if you can spend the recommended hour or more on each step. If you have an interview scheduled a week from now, try completing one step each day. If you have less time before your interview, read and do the exercises in Step One to identify areas you'd like to improve and concentrate on those.

Now let's take a closer look at what you'll be learning in each of the seven steps.

In **Step One** we'll start by developing a short warm-up routine that will get your mind and body in optimum shape to do the interview. The main exercise of this step is a mock interview, a sort of diagnostic test to see what skills you most need to work on.

In **Step Two** you'll do a series of exercises designed to help you remember your personal and professional strengths, including some you may not be aware of yet. Modesty is highly valued in our society, but the job interview is no place for it. Step Two will help you overcome excessive modesty and practice the role of you at your best.

In **Step Three** you'll research the company you're applying to and practice the acting technique of visualization. Imagining yourself in a position is the first step toward making the interviewer imagine you there.

In **Step Four** you'll plan your interview "costume," makeup, and props and learn techniques for making yourself look and feel your professional best.

In **Step Five** we'll deal with stage fright as it relates to the interview: what it is and how to overcome it. We'll then go on to practice techniques of effective communication.

In **Step Six** you'll investigate the role of the other person in your "scene": the interviewer. Understanding what she wants is an important part of getting what you want.

In **Step Seven** we'll put it all together and do a dress rehearsal.

The program ends with some last-minute advice for the **Day Of** the interview and some tips for following up on the **Day After**.

PREPARATION

There are only two things you need before you can begin Step One:

1. A pencil

2. A buddy

The Pencil

A part of using this book effectively involves writing—either in this book, or in a notebook or journal. Don't be self-conscious about your writing. You don't need any special skills, and no one but you will ever read what you write. But the simple act of getting some thoughts down on paper (don't worry whether they're good thoughts or not!) will help you to think more clearly and specifically about what you have to offer a potential employer.

An actor preparing for a role will often write a first-person autobiography of the character. Some information about the character's life will be given in the script, but a lot will be left out. What was Hedda Gabler's childhood like? How did Oedipus spend a typical workday? Writing the autobiography sparks the imagination and calls up details the actor might have overlooked in the script. Writing about a character puts him in perspective, and the same is true of writing about yourself.

We'll ask you lots of questions throughout the book. If you only *think* about the answers, chances are you'll move on before you get to any good ideas, and you'll be likely to forget whatever good ideas you do come up with. Get yourself a new notebook (we'll call it your interview journal) and use it to write your ideas down.

Flash Writing

The technique of flash writing will be particularly useful as you work your way through the program. Here's how it works: In flash writing you don't give yourself time to think. You just write, and keep writing, until your time is up. The point is to keep your pencil moving across the page, even writing down total nonsense if that's all that comes to mind. If your mind goes blank, just keep writing the same word over and over. Eventually you'll get sick of that and something more interesting will come to mind.

Sometimes we'll also ask you to read aloud (just to yourself) what you've written, to help you get used to actually saying what you really think.

Too often we (interviewers, actors, and most other human beings) let our conscious minds overrule our subconscious. Flash writing helps us get past that, as you'll see.

The Buddy

Because many of the skills we'll be working on deal specifically with interpersonal communication, some of the exercises will require you to to work with a partner. We call this, not too originally, the Buddy System.

Think of a friend or family member who might be able and willing to spend some time doing exercises with you. (You might want to promise him a nice dinner after you get your first paycheck from your new job.)

Nothing difficult will be required of your buddy, only about two hours of his time in the course of completing all seven steps, and a willingness to deal honestly and respectfully with you. Make sure it's someone you trust and who knows you well, and someone you believe will honor the commitment of time.

(You may have noticed that we referred to your buddy as a "he" in the last paragraph. This is simply to avoid the awkwardness of a lot of "he or she" constructions. To even the score, "the interviewer" will always be a "she.")

Now for your first writing exercise.

Pick up your interview journal and make a list of possible buddies. Don't worry about choosing the right one. Just list the first people who come into your mind.

_____   _____

_____   _____

Now go back and number them in order of your preference.

PLANNING YOUR TIME

Next, take a moment to choose dates on which to do the exercises. Get a calendar and call the first person on your buddy list. If he is willing to help you, see if you can work out a mutually acceptable schedule. If it doesn't work out, move to the next person on your list. It's even possible to use more than one buddy if it makes scheduling easier.

The chart below will tell you approximately how much time you and your buddy can expect to spend on the exercises for each of the program's seven steps. Use the space provided to design a schedule, or make one in your interview journal. (Of course, this is all subject to change if necessary. Consider it a preliminary working schedule, something to help keep you on track.)

PROGRAM PLANNER

Step	Your Time	Buddy's Time	Scheduled Date	Scheduled Time
Step One	1 Hour	30 Minutes		
Step Two	1.5 Hours	10 Minutes**		
Step Three	1.5 Hours*	Day Off		
Step Four	1 Hour*	Day Off		
Step Five	2 Hours	30 Minutes		
Step Six	1.5 Hours	30 Minutes		
Step Seven	1 Hour*	30 Minutes		
Total Time	9½ Hours	2 Hours 10 Minutes		

*Exercises for these steps may require a little advance planning or possibly a field trip, so leave yourself a little breathing room as you develop your schedule.
**Can be done by phone, if necessary.

Once you have a buddy and a schedule, you're ready to begin Step One.

Warming Up and Jumping In

Acting is ninety-five percent preparation.
If you are ready to act, then you can.

—ERIC MORRIS, HOLLYWOOD ACTING COACH AND
AUTHOR OF *NO ACTING PLEASE*

How Do You Get to Carnegie Hall?

Most actors agree that the surest road to a good performance is a good rehearsal process. While practice may not actually make us perfect, it almost always makes us much better. And the same is true for interviewing: The more you practice, the better you'll perform.

If you're like most people, you probably haven't had enough job interviews to completely master the art. Today we'll begin a structured rehearsal process that will give you the practice you need to achieve a high level of confidence in your interviewing ability.

Blowing Your Horn

Much of the actor's rehearsal process focuses on tuning his "instruments": his voice, his body, his mind, and his spirit. In everyday life, most of us don't pay much attention to developing and expanding the capacities of our "instruments." We play them in one key and are satisfied if they can make a little music when we need them to.

Unfortunately, when the body is confronted with a stressful situation (which a job interview can be for many people), it bears down upon our instruments and makes them sound harsh and out of tune. Under stress, simple processes like breathing can suddenly become difficult; the voice starts to crack, the posture stiffens, and the mind forgets how to respond to the simplest questions. If this is what happens to you, don't worry. With proper preparation and practice, both body and mind can learn to relax under pressure.

The following exercises have helped countless actors overcome nerves, channel creative energy, and access the full range of their performing instruments.

WARM-UPS

These exercises should become part of your daily routine—for the duration of this program and beyond. They will not take more than fifteen minutes out of your day, and the results will astound you. If your interview is close at hand and you're working through more than one step in a single day, you won't need to complete the physical and vocal warm-up routine before each step. We urge you, however, to do the confidence builders. Each is an inspiring break from the hard work of preparing for your interview.

Read the instructions for each exercise all the way through before you try it.

Breathing

Breathing is essential for sustaining life. We've been breathing from the moment we were born and we'll continue until the day we die. Unfortunately, when we get anxious we often forget to breathe properly. Learning to control and use your breathing constructively can be an enormous aid in times of stress. Breathing slowly and deeply can relax your body, clear your mind, and increase your ability to communicate effectively.

WARM-UP #1: Deep breathing exercise
Lie on your back and imagine that your body is melting into the floor. Take a deep breath in and exhale fully. Now, on the next inhalation place your hand on your stomach and see if it expands as you fill up with air.

Keep taking deep breaths until you feel your stomach expanding on the inhale and contracting on the exhale. Close your eyes. Imagine that your body is a hollow vessel and that each breath you take travels from your head down to the soles of your feet.

Don't rush through this experience. This is time that you've set aside for yourself to simply enjoy the feeling of breathing deeply. It should feel comfortable and relaxing. Stay on the floor, simply breathing, for at least five minutes. When you feel that you've experienced deep breathing and allowed your body to relax into it sufficiently, slowly come to an upright sitting position. Stay in this position for at least one minute before getting to your feet.

Check in with your body at various times throughout the day. See if you can re-create this deep breathing pattern (expanding your stomach on the inhale, contracting on the exhale) from a standing position. It may seem strange at first, but it's actually the most natural, efficient way your body has of drawing breath. With enough practice, this proper breathing technique will soon become second nature, and you'll find yourself speaking more comfortably and with greater confidence.

Relaxing Muscles

Tension causes our muscles to contract and limits the potential of their movement. Releasing muscle tension is really quite simple, and feels great, as long as you take the time to do it.

WARM-UP #2: Full body tense and relax

Stand in a relaxed, upright position. Take a deep breath in and exhale fully. Start by stretching your arms over your head, with your fingers pointing upward. When you begin to feel the tension in your muscles, take a deep breath in and hold for a count of five. Then relax your arms and exhale. Continue by alternately tensing and relaxing each of the following parts of your body, breathing deeply all the while: shoulders, hands, lower back, buttocks, legs, and feet.

You can also tense and relax your face. Open your eyes and mouth as wide as you possibly can. Then relax. Now squeeze the muscles in your face as tight as you possibly can, then relax. Repeat this exercise three times.

Finally, shake out your whole body. Imagine that you are throwing out the tension that was trapped inside. Breathe deeply and relax.

WARM-UP #3: Rag Doll

This exercise will clear your mind, relax your body, and help you find a comfortable, straight-up posture.

Stand in a relaxed, upright position. Imagine that your head has become very heavy and let your chin drop to your chest. Now, let the weight of your head slowly pull you to the ground, one vertebra at a time, until you are bent all the way over, like a rag doll. Be sure to release your neck so that it feels loose and wobbly. While you are bent over, gently sway back and forth. Don't forget to breathe.

When you have relaxed into this position, gently begin to roll up—from the back of your knees, through your buttocks, and all the way through your spine—one vertebra at a time. The last thing to come up should be your head. Once you are upright, be sure to take a deep breath and relax your shoulders on the exhale.

Pay attention to your posture now. Are you standing up straight without feeling rigid? If so, walk around the room keeping this straight-up posture. Get used to what this feels like. See if you can find this posture again at another moment in your day. Most people feel more powerful and effective in dealing with others once they've assimilated the straight, relaxed spine into their daily habit.

Relaxing the Voice

Nothing betrays nervousness like a dry, cracked, or shaky voice. When the muscles in the neck get tense, they cause the throat and the larynx to constrict, which can make the voice sound shrill and "pushed." Actors spend a lot of time learning to "open up" the back of their throats so the vocal impulse will have an unobstructed channel to travel from the diaphragm (where the breath producing it begins) out through the front of the mouth (where the word sounds are produced).

We all instinctively know how to open up our throats: We do it every time we yawn or the doctor tells us to say "aaaah." You can teach yourself to open your throat during conversation simply by practicing yawning while you speak.

WARM-UP #4: The Yawn Technique

Say the following sentence aloud: "Neil made mounds of money mining moonbeams."

Now simulate a yawn (or do a real one if you can). Repeat the sentence aloud, beginning it while you are still yawning.

Did the words sound deeper and more resonant even after you stopped yawning? If so, it's because the sounds were unimpeded as they traveled from your vocal chords, through your throat, and out of your mouth. Repeat this exercise three times.

Now say the sentence several times without yawning, but try to maintain that "open throat" feeling. You might find that you need to open your mouth a little wider than you are used to. This may feel strange at first, but soon you'll see that your sound is actually flowing more freely, giving your voice more power.

The yawn technique provides great preparation for freeing your voice for your interview. Try it whenever you can throughout your day. (Yawning during the interview itself, however, is highly discouraged!)

BUILDING CONFIDENCE

The warm-up exercises we've introduced so far have mainly focused on tuning your body and voice. The other "instruments," however—your mind and your spirit—also need some daily attention to prepare them to perform effectively in an interview.

The following exercise, to be undertaken at the start of each day, will help remind you of the things that are unique and wonderful about you. These things may be of particular interest to your interviewer, because they will allow her to see who you are beyond what's simply on your resume. But even if they never come up in the interview, it's important for you to remember what a great catch you are, so that you can approach the experience with confidence.

At each step you'll have three different sentences to complete that will ask you to recall your unique experiences and take stock of your positive attributes. Answer honestly and specifically. No one's looking for the cliched, "And doggone it, people like me" response.

When you're done, read what you've written aloud.

WARM-UP #5: Confidence Builder
Complete these sentences here or in your interview journal.
One area in which I excel is _____
_____
_____

One of the nicest compliments I ever received was_____

_____

_____

People can always depend on me to _____

_____

_____

Get used to thinking and saying positive things about yourself. If you don't speak up on your behalf, who will?

Daily Exercise Tip

A great way to relieve stress that gets trapped in your body is through vigorous physical exercise. In addition to the relaxation and posture warm-ups described on p. 11, we urge you to get some kind of cardiovascular exercise over the course of this program. Start something light (like walking, running, aerobics, or swimming) or increase whatever daily exercise you already do. You'll discover that after your body has been put through a workout, it doesn't have the energy to be tense. Your breathing will automatically become deeper and your muscles more relaxed.

Don't forget: Interviewing is a physical activity. Physical training will give you the body awareness you'll need to perform at your peak.

EXERCISE: *Mock Interview*

Proceeding from the principle that interviewing is a physical activity, it's time to do a trial run. For this exercise you'll need to spend about thirty minutes with your buddy. He's going to interview you for a job.

Begin by writing down some basic information about the company you're going to pretend to be interviewed for. If you have a real interview scheduled, you might want to use that company, or use another place of business that you're familiar with (even your most recent place of employment will do), or make one up. It doesn't really matter.

1. What is the primary purpose of this company? How big is the company? What are the various parts of the company and how do they function to-

gether? Who are the company's customers? Write the basic information on a piece of paper you'll be giving to your buddy.

2. Now do the same for the position. What would be your primary responsibilities? To whom would you report? Who would report to you? Write the basic information on a second piece of paper.

And now you and your buddy are ready to work on a role-playing exercise.

Instructions to Interviewee (That's You):

Your role is simply to come in and be interviewed for the job. Take it seriously and do the best you can. Choose the time and place carefully so that you won't be interrupted. Bring a copy of your resume with you, and do your best to get the job.

When you're ready to begin, hand the book and the information you've written down about the company and the position over to your buddy. The buddy's instructions are below. Don't read them!

When your buddy tells you he's ready, leave the room. When you re-enter, the interview will begin.

Instructions to the Interviewer (Played by the Buddy):

Note: These instructions should not be read by the interviewee.

Read over the information the interviewee has supplied about the company and the position. Your task is to interview the candidate for this position.

Don't worry if you have no interviewing skills: most interviewers don't either! Just concentrate on objectively trying to decide if this candidate is someone you would want to have working for you in this position.

When you tell the interviewee you're ready to begin, he will leave the room and come back in. This signals the beginning of the role-play.

Do your best to imagine that the situation is real, and take it seriously. Greet the candidate and invite him to take a seat. Then proceed to determine whether the candidate is the right person for the position by asking some of the following questions. Just use them as a guide. Don't try to cover them all, and if you think of other things you want to ask, go ahead. Keep an eye on the clock, and don't let the interview run longer than about ten minutes.

As soon as you feel ready to begin, let him know. And proceed!

SUGGESTED QUESTIONS:

What about our company most appeals to you?

What are your greatest strengths?

What do you feel are your major weaknesses?

Why did you leave your last job?

What was your most significant accomplishment in your last position?

What was the greatest challenge you faced in your last job?

How do you handle stress?

What unique qualities would you bring to this company?

What specific training have you had for this kind of work?

What are your long-range career goals?

Tell me about yourself.

What kind of position are you looking for?

Doesn't this job represent a step down for you?

How do you handle interpersonal conflicts on the job?

How would you describe your management style?

Self-Evaluation: How Did You Do?

Now that you've actually participated in an interview, you'll have a better context in which to understand the upcoming material. To get the most out of the experience you just had, it will help to think about it a little and evaluate your performance.

Please take a few minutes to reflect on your experience, and then write about it in your journal for five minutes without stopping. Use the flash writing technique described in "Getting Started" (p. 5). Your writing can include an analysis of how you felt during the process, what you thought was effective in your performance, what you might do differently in the future, etc. Just write down anything that comes into your head in response to the question: How did you do?

Go.

If there's anything else you'd like to add, don't let us stop you just because your time is up. Make sure you get down a good description of how the interview went.

Self-Evaluation: Diagnostic Assessment

Your evaluation of the interview experience will naturally reflect the things you think are important about interviewing. For example, if you wrote about feeling nervous, that implies that you think the ability to control nerves is an important component. If you think it's especially important to make a lot of eye contact in an interview, chances are you wrote about your level of success at maintaining it.

Now we have a more specific evaluation form for you to fill out. This one reflects many of the things *we* think are important in a job interview. Indicate by circling the appropriate response how much you agree or disagree with each of the following statements about your mock interview. Some may be difficult to answer. Just do the best you can.

1. I emphasized my strengths.
strongly agree   agree   neutral   disagree   strongly disagree

2. I gave specific, descriptive answers to questions.
strongly agree   agree   neutral   disagree   strongly disagree

3. I gave examples to support my statements about myself.
strongly agree   agree   neutral   disagree   strongly disagree

4. I allowed myself to control the course of the interview when necessary.
strongly agree   agree   neutral   disagree   strongly disagree

5. I felt relaxed.
strongly agree   agree   neutral   disagree   strongly disagree

6. I appeared to be relaxed.
strongly agree   agree   neutral   disagree   strongly disagree

7. I was confident that I was the right person for the job.
strongly agree   agree   neutral   disagree   strongly disagree

8. I projected confidence that I was the right person for the job.
strongly agree   agree   neutral   disagree   strongly disagree

9. My body language (eye contact, facial expressions, hand movements, etc.) did not detract from what I was saying.
strongly agree   agree   neutral   disagree   strongly disagree

10. My body language contributed to what I was saying.
strongly agree   agree   neutral   disagree   strongly disagree

11. My voice did not detract from what I was saying.
strongly agree   agree   neutral   disagree   strongly disagree

12. I used my voice effectively to contribute to what I was saying.
strongly agree   agree   neutral   disagree   strongly disagree

13. I projected a professional image.
strongly agree   agree   neutral   disagree   strongly disagree

14. I conveyed enthusiasm about the job.
strongly agree   agree   neutral   disagree   strongly disagree

15. I asked substantive questions.
strongly agree   agree   neutral   disagree   strongly disagree

16. The interviewer seemed to think I asked good questions.
strongly agree   agree   neutral   disagree   strongly disagree

17. I demonstrated knowledge of the company and the position.
strongly agree   agree   neutral   disagree   strongly disagree

18. I described the unique contributions I could make to the company.
strongly agree   agree   neutral   disagree   strongly disagree

19. I was attuned to what the interviewer needed to know.
strongly agree   agree   neutral   disagree   strongly disagree

20. I made the interviewer want to hire me.
strongly agree   agree   neutral   disagree   strongly disagree

If you answered "strongly agree" to all of the above, then perhaps you should consider making a career of being interviewed. If not, you now have something against which to measure your improvement as you continue with this program.

These twenty questions cover all the major skills that are necessary for an effective interview performance. We'll address each of them in detail over the course of this program. You might find it helpful to look back at this evaluation periodically throughout your interview training to chart your progress.

Looking Ahead

Some of the upcoming exercises will require you to prepare specific information about your prospective employer. So if you haven't already done it, this would be a great time to call and ask for written materials describing the work of the real organization or organizations where you're planning to interview. Request brochures, newsletters, mission statements, company dossiers—anything you can get your hands on!

For now, all you have to do is read the materials. In Step Three we'll give you some exercises to help you use your knowledge of the company to your best advantage.

STEP **2**

Who Am I, Anyway?

*What good is truth if it's dull and boring? Exciting
truths can be truthful, too. Learn to prefer those.*

—MICHAEL SHURTLEFF, BROADWAY
CASTING DIRECTOR

WARM-UP

Go through your physical and vocal warm-up routine. If you're going
through the steps over a number of days, it's best if you do these exercises
at the same time every day so that they can become a part of your routine.
If you're doing more than one step in a single day and have already completed the daily routine, you can skip these, and go straight to the confidence builder below.

DAILY ROUTINE: Deep Breathing
Full Body Tense and Relax
Rag Doll
Yawn Technique

After completing your physical and vocal exercises, check in with your
body. Can you identify any places where you're still holding tension? (The
most common tension spots are the shoulders, the jaw, between the eye-
brows, and the hands.)

Spend a little extra time shaking out or loosening up these areas. Then take a deep breath and imagine that you are filling these tension spots with fresh air, which will release and relax the muscles. Repeat this exercise several times until you feel the muscles let go.

CONFIDENCE BUILDER

Complete these sentences here or in your interview journal.

The achievement I am most proud of this year is_____
_____
_____

My favorite recreational activity is_____
_____
_____

I really helped someone out when I_____
_____
_____

Now that you've completed your warm-up, you're ready to tackle the main activity of the day: discovering and believing in the exciting truth about yourself. Like all good actors, you'll begin by looking inside yourself, remembering who you are, and exploring who you can be.

"TELL ME ABOUT YOURSELF"

These words can send even the most qualified job applicant into a neurotic frenzy. (*What does he want from me? What should I try to be?*) As we've already pointed out, interviewers aren't interested in hearing you robotically recap your resume. On the other hand, "I was born in a small town in Mississippi" is probably going too far in the other direction. While it's impossible to read the interviewer's mind, it's safe to assume that she wants to hear a combination of specific, interesting stories about your work accomplishments, your personal life, and the kind of impact you hope to make in the future.

Many people have difficulty talking candidly about their positive attributes and achievements. They feel arrogant when they describe past successes or talk about future contributions. Their fear of seeming boastful inhibits them from making a strong case to the future employer about why they should be hired.

Unfortunately, it's very difficult to convince someone that you have a lot to offer a company if you're not willing to tout your own assets. Talking about your strengths in a job interview isn't bragging; it's simply providing the potential employer with information she needs to assess your suitability for the position.

Selling Yourself

Self-confidence is the actor's most precious asset. If you're going to stand up in front of an audience of thousands and demand they pay attention, you've got to believe you're worth paying attention to. While interviewing may take place before a smaller audience, the principle is the same: More than anything else, you've got to believe in the value of what you have to offer.

Lack of confidence is one of the major reasons job candidates get turned down. If you don't have confidence in yourself, how can you expect to inspire it in others?

Consider this scenario: You're selling a Bic pen to someone. You want him to buy it. Which of the two following presentations do you think would be more effective in making the sale?

Pitch #1: "I know this is only a cheap plastic pen, but at least it writes without smudging. I'm sorry that I can't offer you a gold Cross pen, but this is all I have."
Pitch #2: "This is a classic writing instrument. It's inexpensive, lightweight, and gets the job done. Ask the millions of people who use it: Bic offers outstanding quality at a price you can afford."

First, we should point out that both of these statements about the Bic pen are true—they just offer different ways of looking at the product. Obviously no salesperson worth his salt is going to use the first approach, because it would make a potential buyer feel that he was getting something of inferior value. Incredibly, many job candidates try to sell *themselves* in just this apologetic, wishy-washy manner. They think it's the only way to be "honest."

Playing down your strengths in an interview isn't honesty; it's stupidity. Your job is to sell your "Bic pen" with pride—in other words, to talk truthfully about the best you have to offer. Here's an exercise designed to help you do just that.

EXERCISE: "Tell Me about Myself"

When creating a role, actors study the script to discover how they're viewed by the other characters in the play. What other people say about you can be every bit as enlightening as what you say about yourself. In this exercise, you'll have the opportunity to hear some of the good things others might say about you—which may give you some new ways of seeing yourself.

In order to combat the very human tendency to "play yourself down," we're asking you to write an imaginative biography of your life from the point of view of the people most likely to "play you up."

First, we'll divide your life into several time periods:

1. Childhood

2. Adolescence

3. Young Adulthood

4. The Present

(If you're still in your Young Adulthood, feel free to use only three divisions.)

Choose a specific person from each of these periods who knew you well and liked you: parent, teacher, best friend, colleague, spouse, etc. These people will be your "biographers" for the different periods of your life. Record their names in the spaces below.

1. Childhood: Name of Biographer _____

2. Adolescence: Name of Biographer _____

3. Young Adulthood: Name of Biographer _____

4. The Present: Name of Biographer _____

Now in your journal, write your biography as it would be written by each of these people. They probably won't be as reluctant to write about your achievements as you might be, so give them free rein over your imagination. Begin each biography on a fresh page and allow yourself five minutes for each period of your life. Flash write as much as you can in that time.

Now look back over what you've written. Did your biographers bring out strengths you had forgotten about? Did they tell stories that captured you at your best? These descriptions need to be incorporated into the way you think about yourself. Only then can you bring them to the forefront of your self-presentation.

Interpreting Yourself

We're always choosing which parts of ourselves to bring forward. Sadly, many of us are led to believe from an early age that the real truth about ourselves is either the ugliest or most mundane stuff we can think of. As you may have realized during the previous exercise, this kind of thinking is not only counterproductive; it's ridiculous.

An actor must be adept at discovering and using different parts of himself in order to interpret a character to the audience. Your job in an interview is to interpret yourself to the interviewer. That's the *art* in interviewing: presenting an exciting composite of yourself. And this artistic self-creation is just as true as the "you" you're used to imagining.

Your uniqueness as an individual—that which makes you different from any other candidate—is what you must believe in and convey to the prospective employer. It's undoubtedly true that you have some particular qualities that no one else has. You also have a personal vision that is uniquely yours. In other words, only you can play Hamlet your way, so don't try to be Olivier. Celebrate the best that's in you.

EXERCISE: *Identifying Your Assets*
   I am . . .

For the next five minutes, finish this sentence in your journal with as many positive attributes or adjectives as you can think of, like this:

I am . . .
resourceful
highly motivated
a great listener

Write for five minutes without stopping. If you get stuck, repeat the last word you have written until a new word comes to mind. DO NOT EDIT! Ignore the little voice in your head that says you really aren't this great. (You are!)

When you're finished, ask your buddy to create a similar list for you. (This can be done over the phone.) Then have your buddy read his list to you. If he came up with some attributes you didn't think of, add them to the ones you've identified.

Now read the entire list aloud, beginning with "I am . . . " Are you comfortable saying these things about yourself? If not, pick out a few of these descriptions and say them aloud to the mirror (again, beginning with "I am . . . ") until you look and feel natural talking about yourself this way. The more you practice, the easier it'll be.

EXERCISE: *Demonstrating Your Assets*

Next, choose the five words from the list that you are most proud to have attributed to you. It's time to start backing up your claims.

In the spaces below, or in your journal, write down a concrete example from your work or personal life of a time when you exhibited each trait. For example, "I demonstrated my creativity when I developed a successful new marketing plan for the product, including circular flyer distribution and shopping mall demos."

Be specific. Remember: At the interview level, everybody has credentials impressive enough to make the prospective employer want to meet them. How can you stand out?

Your specific accomplishments are guaranteed to be different from any other applicant's and will therefore set you apart. Lots of people may have similar good qualities, but only you have your specific experiences and achievements. Show them off.

Attribute Example #1: I demonstrated my_____
_____when I_____
        (positive attribute)
_____
_____

Attribute Example #2: I demonstrated my_____
_____when I_____
(positive attribute)
_____
_____

Attribute Example #3: I demonstrated my_____
_____when I _____
(positive attribute)
_____
_____

Attribute Example #4: I demonstrated my_____
_____when I_____
(positive attribute)
_____
_____

Attribute Example #5: I demonstrated my_____
_____when I_____
(positive attribute)
_____
_____

Good. This is proof that you are what you say you are.

Now let's look a little more closely at the examples you've given. Did you clearly and specifically describe the *value* of your accomplishments? Was the language you used to describe your achievements bold and active, or modest and self-effacing? Did you write about your experiences in terms of duties you were merely expected to perform, or unique accomplishments that were above and beyond the requirements of the situation?

Avoid being tentative when you talk about yourself in the interview. "I'm probably kind of a somewhat hard worker" isn't going to get anyone's attention. When you describe your achievements and experiences, make strong statements like "My dedication and my ability to stay on a task have enabled me to get many jobs in ahead of schedule." Don't forget: Exhibiting self-confidence in the interview isn't arrogance. It's common sense.

The Language of Action

Good actors make bold choices and trust that the audience will "come with them." They're *active*. (That's why they're called *actors*!)

Too often in life we're primarily *reactive*. We're reluctant to initiate anything for fear that it will be poorly received. We play it safe, hoping to protect ourselves from rejection and loss.

But what are you really protecting in the interview? You can't "lose" the job because you never had it in the first place. And you won't get it unless you can convince the interviewer that you can do it better than anyone else. **Since you have nothing to lose, *play to win*.**

In the interview, you've got to be active. It's your job to describe yourself in such vivid, exciting, and winning terms that the interviewer has no choice but to see you in the role.

Here's a short list of action words you might use to describe your accomplishments in more powerful terms.

achieved	directed	created	coordinated
enhanced	organized	developed	initiated
increased	improved	engineered	built
decreased	generated	devised	transformed
motivated	supervised	solved	managed
instituted	won	produced	strengthened

Go back and take another look at your **Attribute Examples**. Do they contain any of these action words? If you feel that any of the examples you've given could be stated more strongly, do so now in your journal.

Making an Asset of Yourself

Now you've compiled a compelling list of positive attributes and described past experiences where you've made them work for you. The next step is to convince your prospective employers that these great qualities and experiences can work for *them*.

It's your job to know specifically what you have to offer an employer. If you're interviewing in a field where you have limited experience, make sure you've assessed before the interview and expressed during the interview the skills you have that are transferable. You may have more qualifications for a given job than you think.

The following exercise will help you pinpoint which of your skills will be assets to focus on in your interview.

EXERCISE: *Using Your Assets*
Pick the three adjectives or traits from the list you made in your journal ("Identifying Your Assets," p. 25–26) that you feel will be the most useful in the job you're applying for. Identify and describe a situation in which that attribute could benefit your future employer. Fill in the blanks.

Future Asset #1: I could put my _____
to work for you by:_____ (attribute)
_____

Future Asset #2: I could put my _____
to work for you by:_____ (attribute)
_____

Future Asset #3: I could put my _____
to work for you by:_____ (attribute)
_____

Truth in Advertising

The most important thing to remember here is that *all the great things you've written about yourself are true.* You may not be accustomed to talking about them with such assertiveness, but these are the exciting truths that will get you the job. The way to get used to sharing these truths with others is through practice, practice, practice. "Rehearse the role" by using this positive take on yourself in your everyday dealings with the world.

EXERCISE: *Consolidating Your Assets*
Now it's time to put it all together. Write a short statement (no more than twenty words) that summarizes the reasons why a company should hire

you. Use the information you've just gathered to help you come up with a "thesis" that packs your main selling points into one winning sentence.

Example: "I am a creative result-getter with a proven record of increasing sales."

Write your personal thesis here or in your journal:

Personal Thesis

_____

_____

_____

Say this sentence aloud to yourself several times. Believe it.

REMEMBERING SUCCESS

The exercises you have just completed are designed to strengthen your self-image and help you identify what you have to offer a prospective employer. As you probably know, looking for a job is no picnic, and trying to keep your spirits up during the process isn't easy. Whatever your reasons for being in the job market right now, it's extremely important—for your sanity as well as your performance in the interview—to focus on all the good things you've done in the past and all you can look forward to accomplishing in the future. Don't dwell on the negatives; this will only take away your confidence and give you a big headache.

The following exercise will give you an opportunity to reflect on the highlights of your career. Use this time to remember how much you've achieved in your life. If you're someone who's inclined to dwell, this is what you should dwell on.

EXERCISE: *Success Story*

Write a brief story in your journal about your greatest professional achievement.

Choose a specific event or project from which you derived a tremendous sense of personal fulfillment. Things to consider: What did you accomplish? Who benefited from your accomplishment? How did you know it was a success? Include both how you felt about it and the positive feedback you got from others. The more concrete your description of the achievement, the better.

You may want to take some time to decide what to write about. Hopefully, you'll have a hard time choosing among the many highlights of your career. If you're having trouble thinking of anything at all, your inner critic is working overtime and should be told to take a hike. You've surely had a professional moment you were proud of—you just need to give yourself permission to remember it. If you need time to reflect before writing, come back to this exercise later.

When you're ready, spend five minutes flash writing your story, under the title: **My Greatest Professional Achievement.**

How did it feel to remember this accomplishment? Was it fun to write about? Read it aloud. Did you learn anything about your skills and abilities as a result of reflecting on this experience? If so, allow these insights to strengthen your self-image.

During the interview, look for an opportunity to share this story with your interviewer. It's a great example of the kind of contribution you can make in the workplace, and it's what employers really want to hear when they say, "Tell me about yourself."

Practice telling the story. Don't memorize it—this will inevitably make you sound stilted and mechanical. Instead, ad-lib from your memory of what you've written. If possible, tell the story to your buddy or another friend. See if you can communicate the pleasure and excitement you felt as a result of this achievement. The best way to get someone to respond to you with enthusiasm is to be enthusiastic yourself.

TYPECASTING

For me it was the thing every actor hopes for, a part you can play better than anyone else.

—SIMON CALLOW, ON HIS FIRST GREAT THEATRICAL SUCCESS

What's the one part you can play better than anyone else? Yourself, of course. (Never overlook the obvious.)

Fortunately, *you* are the subject of the interview, and this is the part you get to play. The key to successful interviewing is knowing yourself well enough to present "you at your best." After you've spent this time thinking about who you are and what you've done, that shouldn't be hard at all. So relax.

Resume Checkpoint #1 ───────────────────────

> *Now that you've identified your strengths—remembered what's best about you—take a look at the resume you're planning to bring to the interview. Does it support your personal thesis? If you find that some of the language in it is tentative, incorporate some of the action words listed on page 28.*
>
> *Your resume should reflect the best of you. If it doesn't, change it.*

Visualizing Yourself in the Job

If somebody asked me to put in one sentence what acting was, I should say that acting is the art of persuasion. The actor persuades himself, first, and through himself, the audience.

—SIR LAURENCE OLIVIER

WARM-UP

DAILY ROUTINE: Deep Breathing
Full Body Tense and Relax
Rag Doll
Yawn Technique

Before moving on to the Confidence Builder, take a moment to compare how you feel now to how you felt before your physical and vocal warm-up. More awake? More alive? More connected to your body? Ready to move on? Good.

CONFIDENCE BUILDER

Complete these sentences here or in your interview journal.

My greatest personal strength is_____

_____

_____

My   friends   enjoy   my   company   because_____

_____

_____

I know a lot about_____

_____

_____

An actor is trained to project himself into a role so the audience will believe he is a melancholy prince or a redeemed French convict or whatever else the script might call for. By the same token, you must project yourself into the job you're seeking so that your prospective employer can see you in the role.

In Step Two you took stock of your skills, abilities, and accomplishments—those things that make you "right for the part." Now you'll focus on using those assets to convince the employer that she should cast you in the role.

To project yourself into the job there are two things you need to know: (1) a lot about yourself and (2) a lot about the job you're interviewing for. In Step Two you focused on yourself. Today you'll learn as much as you can about the company and how you can fit into it.

RESEARCHING THE COMPANY

If an actor is preparing to perform Chekhov's *The Three Sisters*, he must acquaint himself with the customs of turn-of-the-century Russia. What was a typical education like? How did they treat their servants? What did they do in their spare time? And what exactly is a samovar?

Unless he learns some specifics about the setting, he will be hopelessly unconvincing in the role. The same principle applies to your interview performance.

Giving a confident, convincing performance in the interview requires that you know some specifics about your prospective employer—what the company does, how its employees behave, what the particular "customs" of the workplace are. Researching the company will enable you to ask insightful questions of your interviewer and to honestly determine whether you and the company have a lot to offer each other.

If you're asked why you want the job, you should be able to give a specific, meaningful answer that's based on a good understanding of the company and the position. If you're not asked why you want the job, you should tell the interviewer anyway.

Preparation Is Power

Good preparation can alleviate the nervousness brought on by the interview process. Nothing engenders a feeling of confidence like knowing whereof you speak. So find out everything you can.

Often, the best sources of information about a company are the informal ones—people working in that organization or in others like it who can give you an insider's view of what goes on in the business. If you can think of somebody who might have some knowledge to pass on, give them a call.

OTHER SOURCES YOU MIGHT WANT TO CONSULT:

Company or organization brochures, newsletters, annual reports, newspaper articles

Former or current employees

The sales or public relations department of the company (Don't be afraid to tell them why you're calling.)

Company receptionists (ditto)

Reference librarians

Industry specialists and competing companies

Company suppliers

Standard and Poor's Register of Corporations, Directors and Executives

Dunn and Bradstreet's Million Dollar Directory

This list is geared toward corporate enterprises, and is by no means comprehensive. If you're looking for information about other types of organizations, like law firms, schools, and nonprofits, ask the reference librarian at your local library to guide you to helpful sources.

Fortunately, you don't need to spend the entire day on the phone or buried in a book to get the information you need. Looking through a few good written sources and having a brief conversation with someone in the know may be all it takes to prepare yourself. What you want from your research is a sense of where the company's been, how it got there, and where it hopes to go in the future.

EXERCISE: *Who Are They, Anyway?*

After you've done some research on the company, answer the following questions to the best of your ability, either in the space provided or in your journal.

Who will be conducting your interview? Give name and title. _____

_____

_____

What's the primary purpose or mission of the company? _____

_____

_____

What is the basic organizational structure of the company? _____

_____

_____

How does the position for which you are applying fit into this structure?

_____

_____

To the best of your knowledge, what are the primary responsibilities of the position? _____

_____

_____

What about the position or company most appeals to you? _____

_____

_____

How formal or informal is the atmosphere? _____
_____
_____

What would you describe as the major strengths of this company? _____
_____
_____

In your opinion, what are the major needs of this company?_____
_____
_____

If you were able to think of answers to all of these questions, you're well on your way to being able to project yourself into the job. If you got stumped along the way, maybe you have some more research to do, or maybe you were trying too hard to think of the "right" answer. Since most of these questions can be answered in many ways, don't get hung up on rights and wrongs. Go back and fill in the blanks!

Don't be afraid to come up with your own particular take on the goals of the company and the challenges facing it. These unique insights are what will separate you from all the other qualified candidates.

Yours Is to Question

Now that you've got a good sense of the company and the position you're applying for, you can begin to develop your own list of questions to ask the interviewer. Again, take an active stance here. This is not only the company's chance to interview you, it's also your chance to interview the company. If you don't ask any questions, the interviewer will wonder why you take so little interest in your career and your future.

Ask about what you want to know. Possible topics include the specific responsibilities of the position, what special skills the employer is looking for, who the organization serves, and past approaches to getting the job done. It's probably best to delay discussing salary and benefits until the interviewer brings the subject up or an offer is made. (Too much focus on these issues early on suggests that you're more interested in *taking from* than *giving to* the company.)

It's a good idea to take to the interview a list of questions you want to remember to ask. Feel free to glance at it occasionally. Lists like this are perfectly acceptable in any interview. They're your "cue cards" and they'll help you use your preparation to your best advantage.

Most importantly, when you ask a prospective employer a question, *care* about the answer and *respond* to what you're hearing. Nothing is more off-putting than people who ask questions just because someone told them to. Also, ask open-ended rather than yes/no questions. "What kind of training programs do you have for new employees?" will surely engage the interviewer more successfully than, "Do you have training programs for new employees?" At its best, an interview is a great conversation, so do your part to keep the dialogue flowing freely.

EXERCISE: *Interviewing the Interviewer*

Based on the company research you've completed and the career goals you've defined for yourself, write down five questions in your journal you'd like to ask your prospective employer.

Jot these questions down on a cue card and take them with you to the interview. If you think of others as you continue to prepare, jot them down, too. Look for appropriate moments in the conversation to ask them. Try to space your questions throughout, so that you don't get stuck with a long list at the end. Remember: The interview is an exchange of information between two potential business partners. Be sure you walk away with your important questions answered.

PROJECTING YOURSELF INTO THE JOB

The part of Willy Loman (from Arthur Miller's *Death of a Salesman*) was made famous by actor Lee J. Cobb, who portrayed him as a fallen giant slowly coming to terms with the end of his life. For years afterward, the role remained the exclusive province of tall, sad men. Until 1985, that is, when Dustin Hoffman dared to challenge the traditional interpretation. His Willy Loman was a manic terrier, a man who refused to go down without a fight. Hoffman's unique portrayal won him critical raves and an Emmy award. In short (pun intended), he made the role his own.

Fortunately for the producers of this revival (and all those lucky enough to see his performance), Hoffman did not attempt to re-create the role exactly as it had been done before. And neither should you.

Too often, job candidates allow themselves to think only about what a job *has been*—how it's been performed in the past—rather than what it *could be*. While it's important to have a base of knowledge about how the company and the position have functioned up until now, don't try to fill someone else's shoes. Make the role your own.

Employers value people who can make unique and creative contributions to the organization. The job candidate who convinces a prospective employer that he'll go beyond the current expectations for performance in the position is more likely to leave a lasting impression than the candidate who simply wants to maintain the status quo.

The Expert Problem Solver

Ask not what the company can do for you; ask what you can do for the company.

A sure way to make a lasting impression is to cast yourself in the role of the Expert Problem Solver—the doctor who can cure the company's ills. Job seekers are a dime a dozen, but "answer people" are rare. If you offer effective solutions to problems facing the company, the employer can't afford *not* to hire you.

Can you think of strategies for saving the employer money? For increasing the output of the product? For improving morale in the workplace? For strengthening the image of the company in the community? There are hundreds of ways you can make your knowledge of the company work for you.

Look back at your research answers (p. 36–37) and see if you can think of some possibilities for improving the position or the overall workings of the organization. Write them in your journal under the heading **Ideas for Improving the Company.**

Words to the Wise

Introduce your ideas regarding innovations in the company with great tact. While creative thinkers are highly valued, pushy critics are not. Be sure you mention what impresses you about the company even as you offer new strategies for solving its problems.

The Magic If

If acts as a lever to lift us out of the world of actuality into the realm of possibility.

—CONSTANTIN STANISLAVSKI, THE MOST FAMOUS ACTING
TEACHER OF ALL TIME

The "magic if" is a powerful tool for actors. While it sounds mysterious, it's actually quite simple. In order to believe in the reality of the character's experience, the actor asks himself, "What might I do *if* I were really in this situation?" In this way, he not only personalizes the experience, but also opens up a world of possibilities to explore.

Employers are also aware of the power of the "magic if." Interviewers often give job candidates hypothetical scenarios to wrestle with, such as "What would you do if a client reneged on an agreement?" They're asking you to imagine yourself in the situation to see how you might behave.

As you prepare for your interview, you can make the "magic if" work for you by asking yourself, "What contributions might I make if I were hired for this job?" This kind of question can open up your imagination to the possibilities of the position, instead of limiting your thinking to the reality of what currently exists.

The following exercise will help you get the most out of your "magic if."

EXERCISE: *Future Success Story*

Congratulations! You've been hired by the company you're currently interviewing with. It has been one year since you began working there and your department is thriving. You've done such a great job that you've been asked by your supervisor to give a speech to your colleagues, discussing your innovations and achievements and explaining your strategies for success.

Take a few minutes to visualize yourself on the job and to imagine all the things you've accomplished over the past year. A few questions to spark your imagination:

What was the greatest challenge you faced this year?

What are you most proud of?

How many people work with/for you?

How do you look when you walk into the room to make this speech?

When you're ready, write down your remarks to your colleagues in your journal using the following sentences as a jumping-off point.

"I'm very honored to have been asked to speak with you about

my achievements over the past year. In particular, I am most proud of . . ."

Flash write for five minutes. Don't be modest. Your coworkers are here to learn from your great example.

As you wrote this, did you create a mental picture for yourself of how you performed the job? Did you imagine that you enjoyed the job? Were you able to see the contribution you made to the company?

These are important things to remember when you walk into the interview. If you can truly see yourself in the job, you're likely to make an employer see you there also.

Speak the Speech, I Pray You

A speech is designed to be spoken, and the one you just wrote is no exception. Take a few moments now to deliver this speech to your imaginary audience of colleagues. Just for fun, imagine that the audience is composed of the real people in your life who you'd most like to tell about your success.

Share your enthusiasm about your accomplishments and try to get your audience as excited as you are. Infuse your listeners with the passion you feel for what can be achieved in the workplace.

When you're done, think about the way you delivered this speech. Things to consider: Did you speak with confidence? Did you ever smile during your presentation? Did you notice any changes in your normal speech habit as you did this exercise? If so, try to pinpoint which of these changes made your communication more effective, so that you can incorporate these habits into your daily conversations. (We'll have more to say about effective communication in Step Five, but this is a great time to start thinking about it.) Write down your thoughts in your journal under the heading: **Reflections.**

The Art of Persuasion

To paraphrase Sir Laurence Olivier: If somebody asked us to put into one sentence what interviewing was, we would say that interviewing is the art of persuasion.

Your job at the interview isn't simply to talk about yourself openly and honestly (although it's essential to do so), but also to *persuade* the employer that you're the one for the job. Talk with enthusiasm about your potential within the company and make the employer believe you were born to play this part.

Resume Checkpoint #2

Now that you've learned more about the company and visualized yourself working there, review your resume and make sure it suggests the future contributions you can make to the organization.

Looking the Part

It is always important to me, in a character part, to be able to satisfy myself with my visual appearance. I imagine at rehearsals how I hope to look, but if my makeup comes out well at the first dress rehearsal, my confidence is increased a hundredfold.

—SIR JOHN GIELGUD

WARM-UP

DAILY ROUTINE: Deep Breathing
Full Body Tense and Relax
Rag Doll
Yawn Technique

After you go through your warm-up routine, consider the following questions:

Are any of the exercises getting easier to perform? If so, what about them feels more comfortable? In what way(s) do you think your body has benefited from doing these exercises?

Audio Tape Exercise

As part of your vocal warm-up today, you'll begin a speech exercise that will be completed in Step Five. This exercise is designed to help you build effective communication skills. To get started, you'll need a newspaper and a tape recorder.

Find an editorial that you agree with. Read it aloud to the tape recorder, trying to get your point across as clearly and effectively as possible. Don't listen to it yet. In Step Five we'll ask you to play back and assess what you've recorded.

CONFIDENCE BUILDER

Complete these sentences here, or in your interview journal.

A good decision I recently made was_____

_____

_____

One thing I really like about myself is_____

_____

_____

I'm really looking forward to_____

_____

_____

Actors know that you've got to look the part in order to make the audience believe you in the role. Think of Cyrano without the nose or *Cats!* in street clothes. Who'd buy it?

What you wear and how you carry yourself speaks volumes about the character you're playing. And, as the old adage goes, "interviewing imitates art" (or something like that). If you want someone to see you as a confident professional who can make a strong contribution to a company, you've got to look like one.

The previous chapters have been devoted to creating the role from within—finding new ways to think about your abilities and past experiences, and developing an exciting picture of your future potential to project into the mind of the employer. Now we'll focus on the externals—in acting terms, your costume, makeup, and props.

The Professional Image

While clothes may not "make" the man or woman, they certainly tell people a lot about the person who wears them. A professional appearance indicates that you understand what's appropriate in the workplace. A slovenly appearance, on the other hand, suggests that you don't care how you're perceived by others, and may lead a prospective employer to believe you'll have a hard time fitting into the organization. Whether or not you're particularly attentive to the details of your personal appearance in everyday life, you must make sure you look your best for the interview.

Looking good will do more than impress the interviewer. It'll also enhance your self-esteem, giving you an added feeling of confidence and self-respect. (Try it out: On your next "good hair day," put on your best outfit and go about your daily errands. Take note of how you feel about yourself and how people behave toward you. See if it doesn't give you more confidence and earn you more respect than when you adopt a just-rolled-out-of-bed look.)

Looking the part to get the part is an essential component of successful job interviewing. It will enable you to better visualize yourself confidently performing the job and allow you to project this confident image to your future employer.

Fortunately, looking your best doesn't mean spending hours at the beauty parlor or thousands of dollars on a new wardrobe. The plan detailed below is quick, easy, and cost-effective. In fact, once you've mastered these personal appearance techniques, they can be incorporated into your daily routine with very little effort.

THE COSTUME

When putting together your "costume" for the interview, it's your job to find clothes that are right for the role of "you at your professional best."

The costume is not a uniform. You should choose clothes you like and feel comfortable in. But there *are* a few requirements.

THE RULES ABOUT THE INTERVIEW COSTUME:

1. Your clothes should be well-fitting and neatly pressed.

2. You should dress in a conservative but stylish manner.

3. You should look like someone who could work for the company.

Finding the particular look that's right for you might entail a little more research—maybe an undercover visit to the place of business where your interview will be held or, if that's not possible, a trip to a similar company to see how employees are dressing. Make sure you find out what they wear for meetings and conferences—not just on "casual Fridays." In an interview, you're being judged by your professional appearance, so you need to project a more formal image than the employees gossiping around the water cooler.

The following fashion guidelines summarize the conventional wisdom about professional dress. Of course, you have to find clothes that you're comfortable in: suits that suit you. It can be very helpful to look through the latest issues of magazines like *Working Woman, Esquire*, or even the Macy's catalog to see what style of suit or length of skirt is appropriate this year, and to determine which fashions appeal to your tastes. Avoid trendy fashion mags like *Vogue* or *GQ*, however. (Imitating these models might make you look too hip to hire.)

Costume Basics

Women:

Suits in solid colors or subtle weaves. Navy, taupe, and gray work best, paired with a simple jewel-neck silk blouse. Steer clear of loud prints and ultra-bright colors. No self-respecting actor would let herself be upstaged by her costume, and neither should you. Make sure that you, and not your clothes, are the focus of the interview.

The length of the suit skirt should reflect today's style, leaning slightly toward the conservative. One inch above the knee is the shortest you should venture for the interview, no matter how "in" miniskirts are this year.

Don't attempt to shorten the skirt or do any other alterations yourself unless you have expertise as a seamstress. Regardless of how much you spent on the outfit, an unprofessional tailoring job will ruin your professional look. If your skirt does need to be shortened, ask the tailor to leave a two-inch hemline in case hem lengths go down next year.

Choose well-fitting undergarments and panty hose in subtle shades (natural, gray, off-black) which complement the color of the suit. Avoid jewelry that's too ostentatious, exotic, or noisy (clanking bracelets can drive an interviewer to distraction)—simple gold chains, or a string of pearls and matching earrings are always a sure bet. Use perfume sparingly or not at all.

A small black shoulder purse and low-heeled pumps in good condition complete the costume, making you look and feel like the consummate professional.

Men:

A navy blue or dark gray suit, white button-down shirt, and conservative silk tie is the costume of choice for professional men. You'll be able to wear this outfit again and again in your professional life, so if you don't already own these things, it's worth making an investment in them now.

It's imperative that your clothes fit well; don't skimp when it comes to alterations. Also, pay attention to what you wear beneath your suit—inappropriate underclothes will undercut the professional image you want to project. Always wear a well-fitting, plain white, crew neck T-shirt under a suit shirt. (No logos or oversize Ts!)

Make sure your feet look as good as the rest of you. They should be dressed in thin dark calf-length socks and well-polished shoes.

Accessorize minimally. Avoid wearing any jewelry other than a watch or a wedding ring, use cologne sparingly if at all, and choose a simple belt that matches your shoes.

EXERCISE: *Out of the Closet*

Now that you have a sense of how to costume yourself to get the part, look in your closet. Which of the items described above do you already have? Pull out all the clothing articles you think you might wear to the interview.

TRY EVERYTHING ON!!! Don't assume that the suit you wore to a wedding three years ago still fits, or that those panty hose sitting in your drawer are run-free. Decide what will work as is, and what needs to be altered, cleaned, or replaced. The chart on the next page will help you assess your costume needs.

WOMEN

	To Be Purchased	Great Condition	Needs Pressing	Needs Cleaning	Needs Altering
Suit					
Blouse					
Stockings					
Shoes					
Slip					
Purse					
Jewelry					
Other:					

MEN

	To Be Purchased	Great Condition	Needs Pressing	Needs Cleaning	Needs Altering
Suit					
Shirt					
Tie					
T-shirt					
Socks					
Shoes					
Belt					
Other:					

Looking Good on a Budget (Tips from Starving Artists)

If you find that you do need to shop for some or all of your interview out-fit, here's some thrifty advice. Go to an upscale department store and ask someone to help you find clothes in the most flattering style, size, and fit. Decide what looks good on you and then, unless money is no object, head for the discount stores. They often carry the same brands for up to 50 percent less.

If you decide that the clothes in your closet already meet the interview outfit criteria, so much the better! Even so, you might want to treat your-self to an inexpensive accessory, like a new tie or a pair of earrings, to give you an extra boost of confidence for your interview.

The Costume Parade

The costume parade, that moment when the actor puts his whole cos-tume together and shows the director his final look, is an exciting one for most performers. As John Gielgud observed, no matter how much he's re-hearsed a role, he can't completely become the character until he knows what he'll look like. The same may be true for you.

So once you've chosen everything you're going to wear, put on your whole interview costume and look at yourself in the mirror. Does looking like a professional make you feel more like one?

Move around in your clothes. Practice sitting and standing with ease. If you've purchased new shoes, get used to walking around in them with confidence. As with most things in this book, the more you practice, the more comfortable you'll feel.

Now, hang your outfit in a plastic bag—away from the kids, the pets, and the temptation to wear it elsewhere. This is your interviewing cos-tume, and you'll need it to be in tip-top shape at showtime.

HAIR

Projecting a professional image means acquiring a fashionable, flatter-ing hairstyle that's not too flashy or too severe. Again, look at magazines geared toward the working professional to determine whether your style is outdated (the long-hair-parted-down-the-middle look you wore in college) or overly trendy (sporting colors not found in nature).

Leave It to the Pro

Cutting or coloring your hair is probably best left to the professional. Don't feel you have to spend a fortune; there are plenty of stylists who can make you look good for a reasonable price. The best way to find a good hairdresser is on the recommendation of someone whose haircut you admire—so ask around.

Once you find a stylist, make sure you tell him exactly what you want (or even better, show him a photograph or a picture from a magazine). Be vigilant during the process. There's no going back once your tresses are on the floor, so stay awake, ask questions, and get the cut you came for.

If possible, have your hair cut at least three days before the interview to avoid that fresh-cropped look. Also, get a style that's easy to maintain and ask the hairdresser to show you how to take care of it yourself.

Dyeing for the Role

If you regularly dye your hair, check to make sure the roots and gray areas are covered. If not, dye it a few days before the interview. This will leave you time to shampoo your hair again, getting rid of possible stains and odors left by the dye.

The key to attractively colored hair is a soft touch. Go for subtle tones whenever possible (light ash brown rather than platinum blonde) and look like a natural!

If you're going gray and have considered dyeing your hair, this may be the time to do it. As much as we'd like to deny it, the harsh reality is that most companies are looking for people who project a young, energetic image, and gray hair can sometimes tip the scales against you. It's a sad state of affairs, but you might as well know about it in advance. The decision, of course, must be yours.

MAKEUP

Men: Don't wear any.

Women: Wear something simple that accentuates your best features. If you know what makeup works for you, great. If not, the following exercise will help even the most cosmetically challenged find the right look.

EXERCISE (FOR WOMEN ONLY): *Making Up Isn't Hard to Do*

For this exercise, you'll need to enlist a friend who, in your opinion, achieves an attractive, professional image through subtle use of makeup. Ask your friend to give you a list of the brands and colors of the foundation, eyeliner, mascara, eye shadow, lipstick, and blush she prefers. If she has different coloring than you do, follow these basic guidelines for choosing shades:

Foundation should closely match the color of the back of your hand.

Eye makeup should be worn in subtle shades (olive, taupe, brown, etc.) that complement the color of your eyes.

Lipsticks are best in rich natural tones and lipliner should be a shade darker than the lipstick.

Blush should highlight your cheekbones and give you a natural rosy glow. Some lipstick shades can double as blusher.

Now, look through your makeup kit and see if you have these items. If you're missing any, visit your local discount cosmetic center. Most inexpensive brands of makeup work just as well as the costlier ones. (Just make sure you're not allergic to anything you buy.)

Once you've purchased the necessary items, ask your friend to show you how she applies her own cosmetics. Find a mirror big enough for both of you to work in front of. As she applies each item, copy her. See if you like the effect. Does the way she wears her eyeliner complement the shape of your eyes, or can you find something that works better for you? Experiment to discover what looks the most naturally attractive on you, keeping in mind that less is usually more when it comes to makeup.

When you achieve the total look you want, write down (in your journal) the steps you took to get there. The more you practice this routine, the easier it'll get. Soon it'll take you no time at all to look your professional best.

PROPS

An actor is never fully dressed without his props. What he carries with him on the set is every bit as important as what he wears or how he talks. Poor Yorick's skull in *Hamlet*, Paul Newman's pool cue in *The Hustler*, and the cigars Groucho Marx waved in every Marx Brothers movie are great examples of props that tell the audience a whole lot about the characters who use them.

Your props for the interview should help you project your professional image and, at the same time, enable you to feel relaxed and prepared while you're there. (But leave the skulls and cigars at home.)

PROPERTIES LIST:

Here's a list of things you should take with you to your interview:

2 or 3 copies of your resume—one to keep in front of you during the interview and extras to give to the interviewer if she should request them

A pad of paper and two working pens—to take notes about anything worth recording and—an old actor trick—to give you something (other than fidgeting) to do with your hands

A list of references and phone numbers

Cue cards (or a list)—with job-related questions (see Step Three)

Directions to the interview site

Contact telephone numbers—in case you're unexpectedly detained

A portfolio or attractive folder—in which to carry the above items

Change and extra cash for parking

A comb or brush—to touch up your hair

As always, it's best to think about your interview preparation in the most positive terms. So, instead of seeing this step as a lengthy list of chores, imagine you're treating yourself to a few presents that will make you look and feel great!

Centered Communication

Suit the action to the word, the word to the action.

—WILLIAM SHAKESPEARE, *HAMLET*
(FROM THE ADVICE TO THE PLAYERS)

WARM-UP

DAILY ROUTINE: Deep Breathing
Full Body Tense and Relax
Rag Doll
Yawn Technique

Deep Breathing Challenge

Find a time in your day (in addition to the warm-up) to do some deep breathing. You don't need to lie down for this. Just allow your mind and body to relax as you go through the inhale-exhale routine. Don't forget: Deep breathing is a quick and easy way to slow down your heart rate and clear your mind. So get used to using this technique to help you restore calm in times of stress.

CONFIDENCE BUILDER
Complete these sentences here, or in your interview journal.

I like to read or study about _____

_____

_____

One area in which I've really improved recently is_____

_____

_____

Most people are surprised to hear that I_____

_____

_____

A Lesson from Babs

In his great book *Audition*, casting director Michael Shurtleff describes Barbra Streisand's first Broadway audition, for the part of Miss Marmelstein in *I Can Get It for You Wholesale*:

"She came onstage in an oversize raccoon coat and looked around, way up to the balcony. 'I got to fill this big place?' she asked. Then she sang, and she did fill it up. She dropped her raccoon on the floor for her second number, saying, 'I like it here,' and then she went into that slow version of 'Happy Days Are Here Again' for which she later became famous. That was a lady who knew how to audition, but I suspect her preparation was extensive and very little was left to chance."

Of course, she got the part and it made her a star. But the point is not to wear a raccoon and try to be Barbra Streisand. Here's how Shurtleff expresses it:

"Most important was the communication, all through her audition, that she liked being there, belonged being there, wanted to be heard, wanted to be seen, wanted response."

A Star Is Born

That kind of powerful communication of excitement and belonging is what you need to bring to your job interview. Actors sometimes call it presence; other people call it charisma. But it's not something you're either born with or you're not. In fact, it's something we're all born with! Everybody can learn to project an inviting sense of well-being by getting rid of all the inhibiting habits we've acquired in the years since we were born wailing and crying and demanding that someone take notice.

Actress Sarah Bernhardt, queen of the nineteenth-century stage, said, "An actor cannot be natural unless he really has the power to project his personality." Her point is a great one. Most people assume that their everyday, habitual self will appear most "natural," and to project anything more than humdrum normalcy will make them seem fake. But you can't really be natural unless you let your personality shine through, and that may not be habitual. The most natural thing you can do is to project more of your true personality (the exciting and on-top-of-it one) into everything you do.

In Step Two you spent a lot of time getting in touch with who you really are when you're at your best, sorting out your true self from your habitual one. Today we're going to work at communicating that great self to others.

A Lesson from Bob

A term that theater people use to describe the sense of really wanting to be where you are and projecting a powerful personality is "centeredness." Being centered is the opposite of being scattered. It means you are mentally and physically relaxed and focused, breathing naturally and deeply. Extraneous movements are eliminated, and everything you do contributes to a strong primary purpose. All of you is available for the task at hand.

Barbra Streisand is centered when she's onstage, and you can be centered in your interview. Centeredness is a natural state that only fails to occur when we allow obstacles like nervousness and lack of preparation to get in the way.

Michael Shurtleff has a story about Robert DeNiro, too. It was DeNiro's first crack at a Broadway show, but this time it wasn't an audition: It was an interview. A director had called him in, at Shurtleff's suggestion, to talk about his experience and qualifications for the show.

Even though he was destined to become one of our foremost movie actors, DeNiro almost blew it in the interview. Shurtleff says he "was shy and inhibited, seemed inarticulate, and was generally hidden and unimpressive." Not centered.

Fortunately for DeNiro, Shurtleff had seen him in an Off-Broadway show and strongly suggested that he be auditioned anyway. When he actually did the audition, the director was impressed and he got the lead. He would have saved everybody a lot of trouble if he had just used his acting skills in the interview!

The main difference between Robert DeNiro's situation and yours is that you probably won't have anybody around who's actually seen you on the job, let alone a big Broadway casting agent who's willing to vouch for you. So you won't get a second chance to make that great impression. If you allow your great qualities to remain hidden, you've wasted your opportunity.

STAGE FRIGHT

The main thing that keeps us closed off from others and unable to project our real personalities, both in interviews and in everyday life, is fear: fear of rejection, fear of looking foolish, fear of failure, fear of the unknown. We think that if we don't put ourselves too far out there, there will be less for people to criticize. In other words, as a particularly depressing fortune cookie once said, "If you don't try, you can't fail."

Considering how much power we let these fears have over us, it's amazing how vague and general they tend to be. It's usually difficult for people to put into words exactly what makes them nervous about job interviews. What exactly is the worst thing that could happen, the thing that ties your stomach in knots and keeps you up at night?

Well, that's precisely the question we want you to answer next.

EXERCISE: *Destroying the Destructive Inner Monologue*
What are you afraid of? Most of the fears we have about interview situations are irrational. But if you know your enemies, it's easier to conquer them. This exercise is intended to identify and debunk the irrational fears that are getting in your way.

Write a first-person monologue in which you describe your worst conceivable interview scenario. How bad could it get, in the worst of all possible worlds? This is your chance to get your absolute worst nightmare out of your subconscious and down on paper.

If you need help, use the following sentence fragments to spark your imagination. Then let your fears run wild and write for five minutes without stopping.

I wake up on the morning of the interview and_____

The secretary greets me and_____

The interviewer calls me into her office and_____

She looks like_____

She asks me_____

I answer_____

She looks at me and_____

I respond by_____

She looks at her watch and says_____

I get up to leave and_____

As soon as I'm out of the office I _____

Now write your worst-case scenario in your journal under the heading: **My Interview Nightmare**.

Good. There it all is in black and white.

Now that you've gotten some fears down on paper, read them over. Chances are they fall into a few broad categories. These categories indicate the larger fear underlying each specific one. Categorizing them will help you see how conquerable they are.

Look at each sentence you've written and see if you can identify the larger fear behind it. For example, if you wrote, "As I'm about to leave my house I discover that my only copy of my resume has an orange juice stain on it," you're probably worried that you don't have your written materials sufficiently prepared.

As you reread what you've written, make hash marks in the following list to keep track of how many of your sentences fall into each category.

_____ Insufficient knowledge about the company

_____ Insufficient preparation of your written materials

_____ Insufficient preparation for specific or tough questions

_____ Insufficient time to prepare before leaving for the interview

_____ Poor body language

_____ Poor verbal presentation

_____ Lack of self-esteem

_____ Inappropriate attire

_____ Other (specify)

_____

This should give you a good idea of what you need to work on before getting to the interview. With careful preparation, you'll have nothing left to fear.

Method vs. Madness

Let's continue to examine what you've written. Go back and cross out anything you wrote that is highly unlikely to happen. These may have arisen because of fears you have in other situations, but if you're honest with yourself, you'll realize they're nothing to worry about in the interview. It's time to admit that these fears are *irrational*. Scratch them out completely. Leave nothing visible.

Once you've crossed out everything that was out of the realm of actual possibility—the irrational fears—you'll probably be left with some rational ones. These are the things you're afraid might really happen in the interview.

Rational fears demand rational solutions, and luckily one can always be found.

For example, if you're an especially frequent coffee spiller and you're worried that you'll spill your coffee in the interview, you can simply make sure not to have any.

Some fears can be eliminated right away. Juice-stained resumes can be avoided by making sure you have lots of copies handy, and by not bringing all of them to the breakfast table. If you're worried you'll be late for the interview, go out and buy an extra alarm clock or arrange for a friend to call you early in the morning.

If your fears are mainly about fielding tough questions from the interviewer, here's a little advice. To deal with them effectively, you must answer honestly, with a sincere indication of how you're working to improve yourself and the quality of your work life.

For example:

Question: "Why did you leave your last job?"

Possible answer: "I left my last job because I felt stagnated. It no longer provided the creative challenge I need."

or:

Question: "What do you consider your greatest weakness?"

Possible answer: "I tend to take on too many things at once, but I'm working on my ability to prioritize."

Be forthright but don't go overboard. Candidness is appreciated; self-flagellation is not.

EXERCISE: *Rational Solutions*

Look again at each fear sentence you haven't crossed out, and decide on a realistic way to handle the situation. Write down your solutions in your journal under the heading: **Rational Solutions**.

Even if you're not entirely satisfied with your attempt at counteracting all your fears, you've at least made a large dent in them. A little nervousness will probably remain, but now you're basically prepared for anything.

Of course, even the things you "rationally" fear in most cases are not likely to happen. In fact, the interview will probably turn out to be a perfectly pleasant conversation between two perfectly pleasant people.

So now let's start thinking positively. How good could this experience possibly be?

EXERCISE: *Fostering the Constructive Inner Monologue*

What if this interview were to be the most fun conversation of your life? What would it be like?

Think back to a conversation (with a friend, lover, colleague, boss, teacher, etc.) in which you felt smart and confident—a conversation that really clicked. You're not allowed to say you've never had such a conversation, or that you've had too many to choose from. Think of one.

Why was this communication exciting and satisfying? How did you behave in the interaction? It may be hard to remember, because when a conversation is clicking along we're not thinking about how we're behaving. But try. How did it feel to communicate freely and openly? Concentrate on what you did rather than what it was about the other person that made the conversation fun. Be as specific as you can.

Now write about it in your journal for five minutes without stopping. Flash writing! Once you start, just keep writing whatever comes to mind.

Go back and read what you've just written. This is how you feel and behave when a conversation is going well, when you know you've got something to say and you enjoy saying it. Aren't these exactly the feelings and behaviors you want to re-create in your interview?

Now, if you think that's easier said than done, you may be right. Communicating confidently in an interview can be tough, but don't worry. You're up to the task. All you really need is the right frame of mind.

When you walk into your interview, you're going to encounter another human being. It only makes sense to assume that somewhere in the world there is a person who can communicate with this human being as openly and comfortably as you communicated in the scenario you just related. Take an actorly leap of the imagination and assume that person is you!

Remember, it takes imagination and creativity to really be yourself. At this point you know a lot about yourself when you're at your best, you've thought a lot about the company and your place in it, and you've taken care of how you're going to look. And you've done all these things in a spirit of imagination and creativity.

Now, in that same spirit, let's look a little more closely at how all of this gets communicated to another person.

VERBAL COMMUNICATION

Since we communicate all the time, we assume we're pretty good at it, but chances are we could all improve our verbal communication skills.

Actors know the value of heightened communication. If, like Oedipus Rex, you've just killed your father and married your mother, every word you say and hear is many times more important than usual. The same is true of other potentially life-or-death situations, like the job interview!

Plays are not meant to be read; they're meant to be performed. It's the live interaction of bodies on stage that makes them exciting. Nobody wants to listen to an actor who seems to be just reading his lines. Audiences expect more than that. But what exactly is it that they want?

They want to experience a human being meaning what he says, bearing witness to the truth and importance of his words, and caring enough to get a response from another person. This is another theatrical idea that crosses over into interviewing. You cannot be a disinterested reporter of facts, no matter how interesting and compelling the facts themselves might be.

You have three important communication jobs: to make the facts clear, to make clear what the facts mean to you, and to get a response.

To investigate the ins and outs of spoken communication, we're now going to put you in a situation in which you can play both the communicator and the receiver of the communication at the same time.

EXERCISE: *Audio Tape Playback*

Listen to the recording you made of yourself reading an editorial ("Audio Tape Exercise," p. 43). Be prepared to hate the way you sound on tape. Everybody does. You're used to listening to yourself from inside your own head, where everything sounds a lot different. But try not to judge yourself. (At least not too harshly!) Imagine that someone you don't know is doing the talking and simply listen to what that person has to say.

Go.

Now write your responses to the following questions, playing back portions of the tape if necessary:

What part of the tape sounded best to you? Why?_____

_____

What part of the speech seemed most important to this speaker (who happens to be you)? Why?_____

_____

_____

What was the main point the speaker was making?_____

_____

_____

Were you persuaded to agree with the speaker's point of view? Why or why not?_____

_____

_____

Were there parts you didn't understand? If so, what seemed to be getting in the way?_____

_____

_____

Circle all of the following adjectives that honestly seem to apply to the speaker:

Logical	Enthusiastic	Energetic	Committed
Authoritative	Bored	Boring	Lively
Shy	Powerful	Friendly	Insincere
Knowledgeable	Incoherent	Sincere	Direct

The Good of the Listener

If you answered all of these questions exactly the way you would hope to have an interviewer answer them about you, then you can skip the rest of this exercise.

Otherwise, look over your answers once again and decide what aspects of your vocal communication you would like to improve.

Now, there's a big danger in trying to correct vocal problems. The danger is that your speech will end up becoming stilted and unnatural because you're trying to follow too many rules. **There is only one rule: Always speak for the benefit of your listener.**

You're not talking for your own good. You're talking for the good of your listener, helping him to understand who you are and what you have to say. This of course assumes that you *know* who you are and what you have to say, but at this point in your training you should have a pretty good grasp on both.

The next step is to record the editorial again, this time with a specific listener in mind. It can be your mother or your buddy or the President of the United States. It doesn't matter who it is, except that it should be somebody you can imagine needing to hear the message of your editorial.

Before you record again, look one more time at your answers to the above questions. For now, the way to overcome any problems you discern in your speech is simply to concentrate on making the person you're speaking to really understand what you're saying and why.

Okay, go.

Now listen to the new recording and write your answers to these questions:

What part of the tape sounded best to you? Why?_____

_____

_____

What part of the speech seemed most important to the speaker? Why?

_____

_____

What was the main point the speaker was making?_____

_____

_____

Were you persuaded to agree with the speaker's point of view? Why or why not? _____

_____

Were there parts you didn't understand? If so, what seemed to be getting in the way?_____

_____

Circle all of the following adjectives that honestly seem to apply to the speaker:

Logical	Enthusiastic	Energetic	Committed
Authoritative	Bored	Boring	Lively
Shy	Powerful	Friendly	Insincere
Knowledgeable	Incoherent	Sincere	Direct

Have your answers to these questions improved since the first recording?

You probably noticed some progress, but chances are there are still some things you'd like to improve. The main thing to continue concentrating on is the need of your listener to understand. In addition to that, here are a few suggestions for some common difficulties.

Downward Inflection Pattern

Downward inflection pattern (DWIP for short) is the tendency to let the energy of a sentence drop off at the end. If your sentences start off strong but lose volume and clarity before the thought is completed, you, like millions of other Americans, are a DWIP sufferer.

Listen to your editorial again. If you notice any DWIP, read the editorial into the tape recorder again and this time concentrate on making the very last word in each sentence the most important one.

This is a great trick for maintaining energy throughout a whole thought. It counteracts the worst effect of DWIP: the feeling that the speaker is not particularly interested in what he's saying.

Emphasizing the last word will feel artificial at first, but remember, it's only an exercise. The point is to get used to caring that your listener receive the complete value of what you have to say. Simply being aware of DWIP tendencies usually makes a big difference in a person's vocal self-presentation.

Speaking Too Fast or Poor Articulation

If your words go by too quickly, your listener will not have a chance to understand their full value. The same goes for mumbling. And of course, making your listener understand the full value of your words is your primary concern.

If you have either of these problems, here's a great imaginative exercise that will help. Imagine that your listener is very intelligent but is not very good with the English language. You don't want to sound patronizing, but you need to make sure the listener understands every word. Try it with your tape recorder and see if it makes a difference.

Lack of Persuasiveness

If you find that your delivery needs to carry more of the force of the argument, it could be that you're losing track of the overall meaning you're trying to convey. This problem manifests itself in interviews, too: In tending to the details required by certain questions, some people forget to keep in mind the things they need to be emphasizing about themselves.

One way to strengthen the cohesiveness and power of speech is to highlight the most important words and ideas ahead of time, to help you keep in mind the particular point you want to make with the words. Go through your text and underline what you think are the ten most important words or phrases, then read the editorial into the recorder again.

In preparation for your interview you should mentally highlight the things you want to stress, or write them down on cue cards, so that you're sure to express your important points with commitment and enthusiasm.

Confident Communication

These exercises should help to give you a sense of confidence in your ability to communicate well. If you're not yet satisfied with your progress, find time on upcoming days to try some of the exercises again. If you keep in mind that everything you say communicates something of importance about you, and that your listener must understand it all, just a little practice is all that will be necessary.

As you listen to yourself on tape, continually ask yourself which parts sound the best to you: which parts most clearly communicate something strong about both the speaker and the idea. These are the parts to concentrate on.

Ask yourself how it feels to speak the way you most like to hear yourself. At first it may feel awkward and unnatural, but with a little practice you can assimilate new vocal habits that will ultimately be just as natural—and much more powerful—than your unexamined, habitual way of speaking. Actors do it all the time.

PHYSICAL COMMUNICATION

All gesticulation is not to be condemned, since even all dancing is not; but such only as is unbecoming.

—ARISTOTLE, *POETICS*

Although dancing in the interview is generally frowned upon, it seems clear that Aristotle had in mind not just ancient actors, but modern job seekers as well. Everything you do with your body says something to the interviewer, so make sure it says something becoming.

Ever since the early 70s, when Julius Fast made the idea famous in his book *Body Language*, everyone has been aware that what you do with your body—how you sit, stand, smile, or cross your legs—speaks volumes about who you are and how you feel.

Since everything you do says something, it's important to remember what you want to say. Keeping in mind what message you're trying to convey is much more important than memorizing lists of body language do's and don'ts.

When an actor feels really in touch with a role and what's happening onstage, he is rarely aware of exactly how his body is behaving. If you asked him after the show to tell you what he did with his hands, he probably wouldn't be able to. That's because he was "in the moment," concentrating on the character's needs and interactions. His movements happened naturally because they served the purposes of the character at the time.

This is the state you want to achieve. The lists of dos and don'ts usually just frustrate people and make them self-conscious so that they do the exact opposite of what they should do. When you act as your best self and fully engage in communicating with the interviewer, much of how your body behaves will just take care of itself.

So the objective is to achieve a state of centered, active connection to the interviewer. This has come up before, and we'll deal with it more in Step Six, but now let's try one exercise that specifically helps with the physical aspect of communication.

Mirroring

One of the most common reasons a person gets a job is that the interviewer identifies with the person, sees aspects of herself in the person, thinks the person is "our kind of people." This is one of the most important body language messages you can send: I'm like you and I belong here.

This, of course, doesn't mean you should deny your individuality. As we've said all along, your unique qualities must shine through if you're going to win the job. But remember, during the interview you must concentrate not only on who you are but also on how you will fit into this particular business atmosphere.

If you're interviewing for a managerial position, in most cases you shouldn't slouch way down in your chair and take off your shoes, no matter how laid-back your managerial style. Even if a relaxed style is what the company is looking for, they will only be impressed by one that fits into the personality of their organization.

So during the interview you need to bring out not only those aspects of yourself that are unique, but also those that mesh with the company's needs. Here's one way to do it.

MIRROR EXERCISE #1: *Physical*

This is an exercise that millions of acting students have tried their hands at—as well as the rest of their bodies. It's great for increasing your awareness of another person and for getting you out of your own physical habits.

Note: DON'T DO THIS IN YOUR INTERVIEW! It's just an exercise. We'll talk about its application later.

Read the instructions all the way through first, and share them with your buddy.

Sit opposite your buddy, either on the floor or in chairs.

Now adjust your positions so that you are mirror images of each other. Make sure the position is comfortable for both of you and just relax into it, allowing yourself to eliminate all extraneous motion.

The next step is the most crucial aspect of the exercise: Establish eye contact with the other person and don't let yourself break it for the duration of the exercise. It may be uncomfortable at first, but the act of will that it requires is absolutely essential.

From this point on, everything the two of you do should be done as if in a mirror. If one of you needs to scratch an itch, you both must do the movement at the same time. This requires that all movements be in extreme slow motion.

Once you've established eye contact, the buddy should begin a slow-motion movement, being sure to keep it slower and smoother even than seems necessary. Looking only into his eyes, do everything he does. Follow his movements. See if you can even mirror the "spirit" of what's coming at you. Giggling is allowed, but it must be mirrored. Ideally, someone walking into the room should not be able to tell who's initiating anything.

After about five minutes of this, you can take over the lead of the movement. Just remember to keep it slow and smooth so that it can be followed exactly. At the end of another five minutes, break the mirror and discuss the following questions.

Did you find it easy to maintain the eye contact? Why or why not?

Did you prefer following or leading? Why?

What level of success do you think you achieved in staying together?

What was your level of self-consciousness?

Did the exercise get easier as it progressed?

This would be a great exercise to repeat, either right now or some other time when you're together with your buddy.

As we've said, though, the time to repeat this exercise is NOT when you're in the interview! It would just be embarrassing for all concerned.

What you *can* do in the interview, or any conversation in which you want to intensify the power of your communication, is to subtly mirror the physical posture and attitudes of the other person. For instance, if she's leaning forward slightly, you can do the same. The idea is to use what you learned in the mirror exercise to help you get in touch with the interviewer and to reflect back to her an image of someone who speaks the same body language: someone who could easily inhabit her world.

This can be done verbally as well. The act of paraphrasing what the other person has just said demonstrates that you have been listening and, in fact, actually helps you listen better. It provides you a chance to "reflect" on what you've just heard, and is a kind of verbal mirroring.

Let's take a few minutes to practice this technique:

Mirror Exercise #2: *Verbal*

In this exercise, your buddy begins by making a factual statement about your environment. For example, he might say, "That table is covered with dust."

Your job is then to reflect back that statement and ask a follow-up question. For example, you might reply, "Yes, there is a lot of dust on that table. Are you allergic?"

The idea is to begin every response with a clear indication that you've taken in what the other person has said by reflecting some of it back to him, and then to ask a related question. Have a brief conversation in which you verbally mirror everything that's said to you, then discuss the following questions:

Did you find it easy to reflect back the statements? Why or why not?

Did you allow what you heard to affect what you said next?

What was your level of self-consciousness?

Did the exercise get easier as it progressed?

If you found it difficult to communicate naturally in the exercise, maybe you were overdoing the reflecting. As you move into the final mirror exercise, you might want to try a more subtle approach.

The final exercise will combine elements of physical and verbal mirroring. Part of the trick is to keep your buddy from knowing it's an exercise at all!

Mirror Exercise #3: *The Whole Shebang*
Important: Do not let your buddy read this.

Tell your buddy it's time for an informal chat about the interview process. Encourage him to share his ideas about what works and what doesn't, best and worst experiences, etc. During this conversation, you have two jobs to do:

1. To find out how your buddy perceives the interview process.

2. To subtly incorporate the physical and verbal mirroring techniques you've just practiced.

Use the mirror idea to strengthen your communication with your buddy. Use the same kinds of gestures he uses and reflect back his ideas by paraphrasing, but don't let him know what you're up to!

When you're done, "reflect" on how it went. How did he respond? Did the mirroring strengthen your communication, or just get in the way? Record your ideas in your journal under the heading: **Mirroring.**

If you found that this exercise hindered the communication more than it helped it, don't worry. It may take a little practice to get comfortable with the process.

When mirroring in an actual interview situation, remember not to overdo it. Avoid the monkey-see, monkey-do mentality. Instead, use the technique to strengthen your eye contact, improve your listening, and generate a sense of comradeship with the interviewer.

TAKING IT ON THE ROAD

One objection you might have to some of the work of this chapter is that it's easy to communicate with your buddy because you know him well. The same will not be true of your interviewer. Now that you've addressed the fears that might be getting in your way and practiced some general communication principles, it's time to start practicing your skills in different venues.

An actor will often try out the physical and vocal qualities of his character in public. Meryl Streep is known for preparing for roles that require an accent by speaking with the accent in her everyday life. This helps her to get used to the feel of it in her body, and frees her from having to concentrate on her speech when she's acting the role.

Find at least three opportunities to practice your new communication skills with strangers. Here are some possible places to do it:

the supermarket

the gas station

the bank

the subway

a street corner

Look for opportunities to communicate with strangers, and employ the techniques of clear, direct speech and subtle mirroring to empower yourself in the interaction. This is a great way of continuing your training and keeping yourself in shape for the actual interview.

Affecting the Other

I'm never out there alone, working by myself. . . .
I always need the other person.

—STOCKARD CHANNING

WARM-UP

DAILY ROUTINE: Deep Breathing
                      Full Body Tense and Relax
                      Rag Doll
                      Yawn Technique

Is there any exercise that doesn't seem to be working for you? If so, think of a way to adapt that exercise into something you feel would be more productive.

Have you added any exercises of your own? (A little extra walking or some sit-ups?) If so, good for you!

CONFIDENCE BUILDER

Complete these sentences here, or in your interview journal.

One thing that really excites me is_____

_____

At my best, I am a_____person.

People take an interest in me because_____
_____
_____

Write one more confidence builder of your own:_____
_____
_____

CONNECTION AND COMMUNICATION

Have you ever seen an actor so into himself that he forgets anyone else is on stage? His performance may be technically flawless (he has a great voice, he moves beautifully, he's diligently studied his role and carefully planned his actions), but it's bound to be a bore. He is ultimately ineffective because he lacks the very thing actors must value above all else—*connection to the "other."*

Connection to a scene partner is the key to good acting, just as connection to another person is the key to all effective communication. There's no point in delivering a message unless it's being received. Communication requires that the message sender be aware of what's going on in the mind of the message receiver so that he can adjust his message if necessary and make sure his point gets across.

How can you plan exactly what you'll do and say in a situation without knowing what will be done and said to you? You can't. It's simply not possible and, even if it were, it wouldn't produce very interesting conversation. Yet many people approach the interview just this mechanically. They plan what they're going to say and say it without regard for what the interviewer might need to hear.

Today we'll focus on how you can use your preparation to help you respond to the specific needs of your interviewer. We'll also examine the role the employer plays in the interview, and discuss techniques for **acting on the interviewer.**

Inter-Acting: It Takes Two

Many aspects of the interview process are completely in your control and can be prepared for well in advance, just as many elements in the actor's world (the lines, the costume, the stage blocking) are set long before performance. What you'll say about your skills and experiences, how well you understand the workings of the company, what you'll wear, and how you'll use your body and voice to enhance your communication are all things that you can plan ahead. What's not entirely possible to predetermine, however, is how your scene partner (in your case, the interviewer) will interact with you.

Don't lock yourself into a rote presentation. Good preparation will allow you to improvise your responses based on the specific relationship you develop with the interviewer.

Taking Your Cue

There's no communication, on the stage or in life, unless the speakers are affecting each other. What you're communicating is only effective if it's being understood by the other person. Which means that listening is as important as talking, because only through taking in from the other can you decide what you need to put out.

In the interview, you should have your own agenda but be willing to take your cue from the interviewer. This means being sensitive to her needs, as they are expressed both verbally and nonverbally. Does she need to hear more about your past experiences, or does she want an opportunity to tell you more about the company? Is she giving you encouraging nods and smiles, prompting you to continue with your line of thought, or is she furrowing her brow, indicating that she needs further clarification or that she wants to move on to another topic?

Applying the skills you learned from Step Five's mirror exercises can help you become attuned to the subtle signals given by your interviewer. Pay attention to these signals: If you're attentive to the employer's concerns in the interview, she'll assume you'll be that way on the job also.

The Interviewer's Subtext

Actors deal with both *text*, the words that are actually spoken, and *subtext*, those unspoken thoughts, feelings, and desires that are beneath the words. Interviewers have a subtext of their own, and the more you're aware of it, the better off you'll be.

No matter what the interviewer is actually asking you, her primary subtext is "What makes you right for the job?"

In the last five steps, you've identified many reasons why an employer should hire you: Your past accomplishments prove you're a result-getter, you can make unique contributions to the workplace, you're a dedicated worker, etc. And as we've said before, knowing these things about yourself is absolutely essential for a successful interview. How you'll actually use this information in the interview, however, will depend largely on the specific relationship you develop with your interviewer.

Creating Chemistry

Every scene partner is different. Even if an actor has played Romeo hundreds of times, his performance will change if he finds himself opposite a different Juliet. The specific relationship between the two characters will depend on the particular chemistry the actors have together. Similarly, every interview is bound to be a little different because no two interviewers have the exact same needs or even the same interview styles.

It's your job in the interview to listen carefully to what's being said early on, so that you can determine how to meet this particular interviewer's needs and how to best respond to her style. Then you can begin to build chemistry.

The following exercise will give you practice creating chemistry with different interview "scene partners."

EXERCISE: *Reading the Situation*
Read the following interview scenarios and write a brief plan of action after each one. Don't spend more than two minutes on each response.

As you consider each situation, ask yourself if what you're getting from the interviewer seems to be good news for you (something you want) or bad news (something you don't want).

If you interpret the interviewer's behavior as good news for you, suggest a way to encourage more of it. If you think it's bad news, find a way to change it. For instance, if the interviewer is listening intently while you describe your most recent work experience, you might want to go into greater detail about your specific responsibilities and achievements. On the other hand, if the interviewer's eyes have rolled back in her head, you might want to change the topic or vary the tempo of your speech to resuscitate her.

Now, write a quick response to each of these scenarios. There are no rights or wrongs here—different people will prefer different kinds of interactions, so just answer from your gut.

1. You walk into the interviewer's office and she immediately begins talking about the company without letting you get a word in edgewise.

Good news or bad news? _____

Your plan of action: _____

_____

_____

2. The interviewer says, "Let's just have an informal chat. I'd like to get to know you."

Good news or bad news?_____

Your plan of action: _____

_____

_____

3. After asking you to take a seat, the interviewer doesn't say anything.

Good news or bad news?_____

Your plan of action: _____

_____

_____

4. The interviewer begins the conversation with a joke.

Good news or bad news? _____

Your plan of action:_____

_____

_____

5. The interviewer nervously fidgets with things on her desk while you're describing your past work experiences.

Good news or bad news? _____

Your plan of action:_____

_____

_____

In all likelihood, none of these situations will actually arise (so if your blood pressure just went up, take a deep breath and relax). They were merely intended to open your mind to the wide range of personalities you may encounter and, more importantly, to prepare you to take an active stance in the interview no matter who you're dealing with.

Performing Actions

Characters in plays and movies always want something from each other. Maybe they want love, maybe they want money. They may even want gainful employment.

Whatever a character wants, it's the actor's job to try to get it. This is called pursuing an objective, and he does it by performing a series of *actions* on his scene partner.

By "actions" we don't necessarily mean anything physical. An actor's action might be to reassure, to plead, to seduce, or to amuse the other character. Any strong verb will do.

In the interview, you have an objective (to get the job) and the only way to achieve it is by performing an action on the interviewer. You also must assess whether that action is helping you achieve the objective. If not, change your action. Be flexible enough to modify what you're doing in order to more successfully affect the interviewer.

Here are some powerful actions you can perform in the interview:

Solve a company problem

Convince the employer that you will be an asset to the company

Win the employer's confidence

Sell yourself

Create a need for your expertise

Facilitate interesting discussion

Overcome objections

Gather information about the position

Demonstrate your potential value

Assess whether you want to work for the company

Note that all the actions we've listed are about *doing* something—not *being* something. To be likable isn't in your control (how do you know what the interviewer likes?), but to facilitate interesting conversation is (and this will probably make the interviewer like you). Also, it's best to think of actions in positive terms: to elicit a favorable response is more active than to not make a mistake.

Now take a moment to think of three more possible actions of your own, and add them to the list:

1._____

2._____

3._____

Don't waste your time memorizing this list. You'll probably do most of these things naturally in the course of the interaction, anyway. The list is

simply here to remind you how active you can be. So, don't just sit there—
do something!

Lend Them Your Ears

Listening is an action, too. In fact, it's one of the most powerful things
you can do in an interview.

Active listening is more than simply hearing: It's paying attention to
and being affected by what's said to you.

Nonlistening occurs when you're mentally rehearsing what you'll say
next while the other person is talking. If your brain is consumed with your
own memorized lines, you'll never be able to take in what's coming at you
from the other person.

What gets in the way of listening in the interview? Nine times out of
ten, it's nervousness (that old fiend!). Job candidates are often so anxious
about making a good impression that they forget to listen. They never stop
talking for fear the interviewer will think they have nothing to say for themselves. Or else they sit catatonically while the interviewer is talking, giving
no indication that they're receiving the messages.

Effective listening is just as important as effective speaking. Fortunately,
as with most things in this book, it's something you can train yourself to do.
The verbal mirror you practiced in Step Five required you to paraphrase
what you'd heard, and then connect this thought to your own experience.
You became an active listener, reflecting back what had been said to you.
Therapists use this technique all the time to let their clients know they've
been listening, and it'll work just as well for you in the interview situation.

More tips for active listening:

Don't be afraid of silence. A "thinking pause" after the interviewer has spoken will let her know you were listening and, at the same
time, give you a moment to collect your thoughts and prepare a dyna-
mite response.

Stay connected. While the interviewer is talking, respond nonverbally to what she's saying. Nodding your head and smiling are probably the
two easiest ways to let her know you've gotten the message.

Ask for clarification. If you're confused by a question, don't be afraid to ask the interviewer what she means. Also, if she asks you something very broad ("Tell me about your life"), find out which part of that answer she's most interested in hearing. ("Would you like me to begin with my recent professional experiences?")

Use what you've heard. If the interviewer has raised particular concerns, respond to them directly, even if they are off the topic you've been discussing. Again, be flexible and take your cue from her.

THE VIEW FROM THE OTHER SIDE OF THE DESK

What You Should Know about the Interviewer

Interviewers have a role to play too, and in most cases it's not their favorite. The person sitting across the desk from you probably has absolutely no training in the art of interviewing. She desperately wants to hire the best candidate and knows a poor choice could have grave consequences. So don't be surprised if she's more nervous than you are.

The more you put the interviewer at ease, the better off you'll be. You can help her feel comfortable by giving her encouraging nods and whenever possible, making her feel you speak her language. It's important to let her know you're on the same wavelength.

Out of Your Head

In the acting world, to be "in your head" means to be self-conscious— debilitated by your awareness of how you look or your fears about what the audience thinks of you. Good actors know that the best way to get "out of your head" is to get into someone else's. And the same is true for the interview.

Your focus should be on how you can solve the interviewer's problem or fulfill her need. If you put all your energy there, you won't have any left to agonize over how you look or how you sound.

In the following role-reversal exercise, you'll put yourself in the interviewer's shoes and as a result, gain valuable insights about the view from the other side of the desk.

EXERCISE: *The Role-Reversal Interview*

In this exercise, you'll be the employer and your buddy will be the job candidate.

Ask your buddy to pick a job he feels qualified to apply for. Have him describe the position and the company to you (he can use a real one or make one up) and then fill in the following information for yourself.

What does the company do?_____

_____

_____

How big is it?_____

_____

_____

What are the primary duties of the position? _____

_____

_____

Next, take the following list of ten commonly asked interview questions and conduct a twenty-minute interview with your buddy to determine his suitability for the job. Feel free to add your own questions and follow-ups to the list.

Pay special attention to his verbal and nonverbal behavior. Is he speaking in an enthusiastic manner? Does his body seem relaxed? Is he giving you informative, helpful answers to your questions?

Shortly after completing the role reversal use the evaluation form on the next page to assess the effectiveness of your buddy's performance in the interview. (Note: The evaluation should be kept private. It's a learning tool for you, and you'll want to be totally candid in your assessment.)

INTERVIEW QUESTIONS (TO BE ASKED IN THE ROLE-PLAYING EXERCISE):

1. What about our company most appeals to you?

2. What are your greatest strengths?

3. What do you feel are your major weaknesses?

4. Why did you leave your last job?

5. What was your most significant accomplishment in your last position?

6. What was the greatest challenge you faced in your last job?

7. How do you handle stress?

8. What unique qualities would you bring to this company?

9. What specific training have you had for this kind of work?

10. What are your long-range career goals?

OPTIONAL QUESTIONS:

Tell me about yourself.

What kind of position are you looking for?

Doesn't this job represent a step down for you?

How do you handle interpersonal conflicts on the job?

How would you describe your management style?

EVALUATION FORM

INTERVIEW ROLE-REVERSAL ASSESSMENT (TO BE COMPLETED AFTER THE ROLE-PLAYING EXERCISE):
Please think about the following statements and indicate how much you agree or disagree with them. Circle the appropriate response.

1. The candidate emphasized his strengths.
strongly agree   *agree*   *neutral*   *disagree*   *strongly disagree*

2. The candidate gave specific, descriptive answers to questions.
strongly agree   *agree*   *neutral*   *disagree*   *strongly disagree*

3. The candidate appeared to be relaxed.
strongly agree   *agree*   *neutral*   *disagree*   *strongly disagree*

4. The candidate projected confidence.
strongly agree   *agree*   *neutral*   *disagree*   *strongly disagree*

5. The candidate used effective body language (eye contact, facial expression, hand movements, etc.).
strongly agree   *agree*   *neutral*   *disagree*   *strongly disagree*

6. The candidate was enthusiastic about the job.
strongly agree   *agree*   *neutral*   *disagree*   *strongly disagree*

7. The candidate asked substantive questions.
strongly agree   *agree*   *neutral*   *disagree*   *strongly disagree*

8. The candidate demonstrated knowledge about the company and position.
strongly agree   *agree*   *neutral*   *disagree*   *strong disagree*

9. The candidate described the unique contributions he could make to the company.
strongly agree   *agree*   *neutral*   *disagree*   *strongly disagree*

10. The candidate made me want to hire him.
strongly agree   agree   neutral   disagree   strongly disagree

Director's Notes

After you've completed the evaluation form, write brief answers to the following questions:

What was his greatest strength in the interview?_____
_____
_____

What seemed to be an area of need in his self-presentation?_____
_____
_____

What advice would you give him to help him overcome these weaknesses?_____
_____
_____

What behaviors did he demonstrate that you would like to use in your own interview?_____
_____
_____

What would you have done differently?_____
_____
_____

What was the most memorable thing he did or said?_____
_____
_____

Why did this particular thing strike you? Was it the content of the story, the presentation, the words he used to describe it, the manner in which he discussed it?_____
_____
_____

Actor's Notes

Briefly answer the following questions about your experience as the interviewer:

What did you find most interesting about this role?_____
_____
_____

Did you want the candidate to do well? Why?_____
_____
_____

Compare this experience to the mock interview you did at the beginning of this program. In which setting did you feel more confident or powerful? Why?_____
_____
_____

If you felt more confident as the interviewer, answer the next two questions.

How was this confidence reflected in your body?_____
_____
_____

How do you think you might capitalize on these feelings when the roles are reversed? In other words, which of the thoughts and behaviors you experienced as the employer can you imagine carrying over to your actual interview?_____
_____
_____

Using Your Experience

When you saw through the eyes of the interviewer, did you learn anything about her needs, wants, and point of view?

List three things about your experience as the interviewer that you should remember when you walk into your job interview.

1. _____

2. _____

3. _____

DEBUNKING POPULAR MISCONCEPTIONS

The interviewer is against me.

The interviewer knows the "right" answer to every question she asks.

The interviewer is not a human being.

Hopefully, your experience as the interviewer proved these assumptions to be as ridiculous as they are irrational. The interviewer wants to like you. If she does, she can hire you and be finished with this time-consuming, nerve-racking process. So, see her as a real person and give her the chance to see you that way too.

Putting It Together

*Choose what you're going to do and do it with ab-
solute conviction, and something will happen.*

—STAGE AND FILM ACTOR ROBERT JOY

WARM-UP

DAILY ROUTINE: Deep Breathing
Full Body Tense and Relax
Rag Doll
Yawn Technique
Spend a little extra time today on whichever exercise you like best.

CONFIDENCE BUILDER

We're not going to ask you to write any new ones today. Instead, go
back and read the Confidence Builders you've already written and gloat
about what a great catch you are!

It's taken a lot of work to reach the last step of this program. To refresh
your memory, here's what you've done:

- You've participated in a diagnostic interview and assessed your interviewing skills.

- You've discovered new, positive ways of looking at yourself and your accomplishments.

- You've researched the company and creatively explored your potential place in it.

- You've prepared your costume and props.

- You've practiced the art of clear and forceful communication.

- You've examined and practiced the skill of affecting another person.

Along the way, you've also incorporated a physical warm-up into your daily routine, gotten used to the idea of self-affirmation, and reviewed your resume.

With all that under your belt, it's now time to focus on the details of the actual interview scenario. Today is the day we look at what happens during this "scene." Then we'll do a dress rehearsal.

THE INTERVIEW SCENE

Here's a basic outline of the plot:

1. You walk in and you and the interviewer greet one another.

2. You engage in a little chitchat.

3. You discuss the purpose of the interview.

4. You have a conversation in which you both ask and answer questions.

5. You discuss what the next step will be.

6. You go home.

Not very exciting on the page, but neither is *Indiana Jones and the Temple of Doom*. It will take the interaction of live individuals to give it some spark.

By the way, please don't waste any time memorizing this sequence. For the most part it will happen automatically. And besides, the stages of the interview aren't really what's important.

What's important is that you be yourself—your well-dressed, capable, knowledgeable, effective communicator self. As our great teacher Stanislavsky once said, "Always and forever, when you are on stage, you must play yourself." And *how* you play yourself in the best possible way is exactly what you've been practicing.

The Big Picture

Now is the time to put your training in context. We're no longer thinking about details. We're ready for the big picture. Your training is over.

At this point in your preparation, with the actual interview right around the corner, the tendency is to dwell on all the things you haven't achieved. This is because you're now aware of how much there can be to think about, so it's hard not to think about it all.

By the time a production reaches its final dress rehearsal, the actors (one hopes) are not thinking about where to move or what to say. That stuff is already taken care of. It's become part of the actor's subconscious. His conscious brain is concerned only with playing the action of the scene: achieving the character's objective.

If you've done the last six steps, you have by now achieved a similar state of readiness, even if you're not aware of it. You know the character you're playing. You know the situation the character is in. You know how the character talks. This is because the character is, after all, you. You at your best, the way you've learned to play yourself.

So, because of your good preparation, there's a lot you know and a lot you can do. Focus on that. Ignore what you feel you don't know and can't do.

IMPORTANT PRINCIPLE: The audience sees only what's there, not what's not.

The interviewer is not out to trap you. She wants to find out what you know, not what you don't. So rejoice in what you know! Your training will hold you in good stead. All you have to do is trust it.

Being in the Moment

The interview, like many other scenes from a play or from life, is primarily about creating a positive human relationship. Instead of worrying about getting the job, concentrate on meeting the person. It will make getting the job a lot easier.

Allow yourself to be in the moment throughout the interview. Don't be ahead of the moment ("Oh, god, what will she ask next?") or behind it ("Oh, god, I can't believe I just said that."). Allow your training to empower you.

Take your cues from the interviewer. Remember that you're not alone: The presence of another person makes conversation a lot easier! Focus on the needs of the interviewer, not on your own. Find out what she wants from you, and help her to see how you can provide it. Remember, keeping in mind the good of your listener will encourage her to keep yours in mind.

Nothing can go wrong. You've already debunked most of your fears, right? That's not to say unforeseen things will not happen. They probably will. It's improvisation, and you're prepared for it.

Remember to use the interviewer as a resource. If she asks a difficult question, maybe she can help you with it by being more specific or giving an example. If you ask for that kind of help, she'll know you're interested in giving the best answer you can. Feel free to probe and redirect. Find out what you need to know in order to help her out as much as possible.

You are now prepared to leave the interviewer with vivid images of who you are and how you will solve her problem by being the person for the job. If you feel like reinforcing that preparation by looking back over your written responses to the exercises you've done so far, now's the time to do it.

DRESS REHEARSAL: *The Mock Interview*

Actors approach the "final dress" as an exciting opportunity to put all the elements of a production together and begin "living the role" just before opening night. It's a crucial stage of the process, and also a lot of fun. Here's how to orchestrate your own final dress.

First of all, in order to make this a real dress rehearsal, it might be a good idea to put on your interview costume.

Then you'll need to prepare some information for your buddy, who will act as the interviewer.

On a piece of paper write a brief description of the company to which you are applying and the position that you are seeking.

Give this description, along with your resume and the prepared questions on the next page, to your buddy and allow him to review the materials for a few minutes.

Imagine that you have been scheduled for a thirty-minute interview. Follow the same protocol as you did during the mock interview in Step One, leaving the room and re-entering to signal the beginning of the interview. Treat this as seriously as you would the real thing. Introduce yourself and allow the interviewer to take it from there.

Keep in mind all the positive things you know about yourself and how you could fit into this company; remember to heighten your communication and subtly mirror the interviewer's body language; project sincerity, confidence and enthusiasm; and, most importantly, relax and enjoy yourself. You're superbly prepared.

When your time is almost up, be sure to notify your interviewer that you only have a few minutes left, and ask if there is anything else he would like to discuss. Also, allow yourself time to bring up anything you haven't had an opportunity to talk about, and to indicate your interest in the position.

When you're finished with the exercise, take a little break, then turn the page for further instructions.

INTERVIEW QUESTIONS (TO BE ASKED IN THE ROLE-PLAY):

1. Why do you want to work for us?

2. It seems as though you may be overqualified for this position.

3. Do you prefer working with others or on your own?

4. Why did you leave your last job?

5. What was your most significant accomplishment in your last position?

6. What was the greatest challenge you faced in your last job?

7. How do you define success?

8. Give an example of your leadership skills.

9. What specific training have you had for this kind of work?

10. What are your greatest strengths?

OPTIONAL QUESTIONS:

Tell me about yourself.

What kind of position are you looking for?

What are your long-range career goals?

How do you handle interpersonal conflicts on the job?

How do you handle stress?

How would you describe your management style?

The Good News

We're not going to ask any specific questions about this one. Now is not the time for little details.

The most valuable thing you can do for yourself now is to think of every good thing that happened during your mock interview, especially in terms of your progress from Step One. Think about what's there, not about what's not. Dwelling on negatives is strictly forbidden at this stage.

Now get all the good stuff down on paper. For at least five minutes, write everything that comes into your head in response to this question:

What was good about what you just did?

Now, just two more things to do:

ON-SITE REHEARSAL

There was really only one thing keeping your mock interview from really being a dress rehearsal: You didn't do it on the set.

If at all possible, get yourself to the site of the interview, not to practice anything there but just to check it out. This could save you a lot of heartache on the day of the interview.

The purpose of this trial run is to make sure you know exactly where the place is, find out exactly how long it takes you to get there, check out the parking situation, etc. That's all. It will keep you from being late or unduly hassled when you arrive, and that can make a big difference in your mental preparation.

And finally:

THE TREAT-YOURSELF EXERCISE

This is the most important exercise in this book. If you're at all tempted to skip it, don't even think about it.

There's one big thing about being an actor that does not apply to job applicants. Actors get applause; job applicants don't.

So, since there's nobody there to applaud your completion of a grueling program, you have to do something nice for yourself. It's required. It's also a great way to relieve stress and to remind yourself that you're worthy of special treatment.

Here are some suggestions:

Take a bubble bath

Get a massage

Go out for a delicious meal

Get someone to cook you a delicious meal

Take a walk in a scenic area

Read a short story

Buy yourself some fresh flowers

Rent a favorite old movie

Take a nap

Call someone you miss

Have a fattening dessert

Or do any other special thing you would enjoy

Remember, you must do at least one of these things today in order to consider the program completed.

Of course, that's just the minimum requirement. It's best to do them all.

Day Of

Any actor who claims he's not frightened on openings just isn't telling the truth.

—LYNN FONTANNE

"PLACES, PLEASE!"

That's your cue to do your last-minute preparations and get to the stage.

You've done a huge amount of rehearsal and now it's the day of the real interview: your opening night. Chances are, despite your preparation, you're a little nervous.

That's a good thing. If you were totally relaxed, you'd be asleep. That probably would not make for a good interview. Besides, employers and their decision makers understand that doing a job interview can be stressful. They won't hold nervousness against you, as if you ought to be somehow superhuman. It's a sign that you're taking the opportunity seriously.

And you can actually turn nervousness to your advantage. Channel the extra energy into the action of the interview. When your heart is pounding just a bit faster, your brain is getting more blood! You're more alert and actually smarter than usual! Rejoice!

LAST-MINUTE NOTES

Here are a few tips to help you perform at your best on the day of your interview:

Allow yourself plenty of time to get ready before leaving for the interview.

Pay special attention to your regular warm-up routine today. In addition to getting you physically prepared, it will help lessen any anxiety you might be feeling. Do it as close to the time of the interview as possible.

Take your time getting dressed, and be sure you have everything on your list of "props" (p. 52–53). Make certain you look your best so that you'll feel your best.

Be "in character" from the moment you leave the house. You're your best self, ready to make your best impression on everyone from your neighbors to the company secretary to the interviewer herself. If you squander your time in the wings, you won't be ready when you get onstage.

Arrive a few minutes early and use the time to review your resume and to remind yourself of all the great things it doesn't say. Dwell on what you have to offer.

An old actor's trick for the few moments right before curtain is to think about a favorite line or moment from the play: the thing he can't wait to get out there and do. Do the same for yourself. Concentrate on your best quality and how much they're going to love hearing about it!

Finally, know that you are now in the best possible physical and mental shape to succeed in this interview. Enjoy yourself. You know what you have to offer. Now all you have to do is offer it.

Day After

*Every path taken from the first reading through clos-
ing night, whether finally used or not, is enriching,
deepening, layering.*

—ACTOR TOM HULCE

CONGRATULATIONS! You've completed an interview, and
that's no easy task.

Now what?

Well, first you need to record a few details so that you can do a proper
follow-up. Make sure you have the correct names and spellings of everyone you met with and send a thank-you letter immediately. Next, spend a
little time thinking about the experience you just had.

LOOKING BACK

After a play closes, the production staff and sometimes the cast will
get together for what is unfortunately known as a post mortem. This is a
meeting to dissect the production, to analyze what worked and what didn't,
to see what lessons can be learned for the future. During the run, everyone was in the moment, consumed with the immediate concerns of get-

ting and keeping the production on its feet. Afterward is the time for reflection.

The same is, of course, true of your interview. During it, you weren't analyzing it. You were doing it.

But now that it's over, it will help to take a few moments to think about how it went for one very good reason: You may have to do it again.

Julie Andrews performed the role of Eliza Doolittle in *My Fair Lady* on Broadway to enormous critical acclaim. Rarely has there been a more impressive "audition," yet she lost the role in the movie to Audrey Hepburn. Moral: You can never really know what they're looking for.

If you give a great performance in the interview, you'll maximize your chances of getting the job. However, you don't have control over the results. Sometimes the interviewer is looking for qualities, skills, or experiences that are completely different from yours. This does not mean you have failed. In fact, you've probably learned that the job wasn't right for you.

Professional actors go from audition to audition and never put all their eggs in one basket. To become overly invested in any potential role will most often lead, through no fault of your own, to heartbreak—so you learn to avoid emotional involvement. That means move on.

Look at it this way: At the very least, every interview is a great dress rehearsal for the next one. Use what you've learned from the experience to help you prepare for the next time you have to do it.

The best way to assess how well the interview went is through a little flash writing.

EXERCISE: *The Reviews Are In*

Think about what went well and what didn't. Write in your journal for at least five minutes without stopping. What would you do the same in your next interview? What would you do differently? Did you present yourself in the best possible light? Did you communicate well?

How did you do?

LOOKING AHEAD

As you continue your job search, keep this book handy. Continue your daily warm-up, and periodically review what you've written throughout the book and in your journal. Of course you can always redo the exercises. The more you practice, the more you will improve.

We hope this rehearsal program will make life a little easier as you pound the pavement. And may you soon find yourself happily starring in the job of your dreams.

Notes

Notes

Notes

Notes

Notes

Notes

Notes